COOKE COUNTY

Then & Now

Cooke County Courthouse as viewed from the north and west
late in the year 2003.
© 2003 Timothy L. Parks

Books by Timothy L. Parks

Glen Canyon Dam
(Arcadia Publishing 2004)

Poker Games, Pillow Shams and Parched Prairies
(Zone Press, 2nd Edition 2004; added material, Forword
and Afterword by Timothy L. Parks)

Cooke County Then & Now
(Zone Press, 2006)

Turn of the century California Street as seen looking east, just across Rusk.
An era long since past, but not so easily forgotten as can be seen in
the later, contrasting image of 2006.

Courtesy of StarrBooks

Looking east up California Street so named
from its rudimentary beginnings as the
Old California Trail.
© 2006 Timothy L. Parks

COOKE COUNTY
Then & Now

TIMOTHY L. PARKS

EDITED BY:
KATHIE A. PARKS
JIM O. ROGERS

ZONE PRESS

Denton, Texas

Cooke County
Then & Now

Parks, Timothy L.
First Edition

Paratroopers Invade Airport - First appeared in the December 12, 2002 issue of the Journal of North Texas

Margaret Donates Glass - First appeared in the December 26, 2002 issue of the Journal of North Texas

NASCOGA - First appeared in the March 11, 2004 issue of the Journal of North Texas

Kiowa Indian Rain of 1868 - First appeared in the April 1, 2004 issue issue of the Journal of North Texas

A Great American - First appeared in the April 15, 2004 issue of the Journal of North Texas

Three Faces of The Turner Hotel - First appeared in the April 29, 2004 issue of the Journal of North Texas

Rain & Sand - First appeared in the May 27, 2004 issue of the Journal of North Texas

Believe It Or Not - First appeared in the June 10. 2004 issue of the Journal of North Texas

Chainsaw Sculpture - Symbol of Freedom - First appeared in the July 1, 2004 issue of the Journal of North Texas

Fish Creek Lodge - First appeared in the July 1, 2004 issue of the Journal of North Texas

Through Rain, Sleet or Snow - First appeared in the July 15, 2004 issue of the Journal of North Texas

My Name is Old Glory - First appeared in the July 29, 2004 issue of the Journal of North Texas

Two Brothers in the 86th Blackhawk Infantry Division at Camp Howze (part 1) - First appeared in the August 26, 2004 issue of the Journal of North Texas

Two Brothers in the 86th Blackhawk Infantry Division at Camp Howze (part 2) - First appeared in the September 16, 2004 issue of the Journal of North Texas

Ye Gainesville Towne - First appeared in the September 30, 2004 issue of the Journal of North Texas

Taps - First appeared in the October 15, 2004 issue of the Journal of North Texas

Death Letter - First appeared in the November 29, 2006 issue of the Journal of North Texas

The Woman of Tomorrow - First appeared in the November 12, 2004 issue of the Journal of North Texas

Remember Them - First appeared in the November 26, 2004 issue of the Journal of North Texas

First Snow - First appeared in the November 26, 2004 issue of the Journal of North Texas

Christmas in Gainesville - December 23, 2004 issue of the Journal of North Texas

Sante Fe Depot - First appeared in the January 13, 2005 issue of the Journal of North Texas

Printed in the United States of America
ISBN:0-9777558-1-9

Dedication

For the men and women of Cooke County
who have served in the military defending
our country both in times of peace and of war.
And for those who still do.

Table of Contents

Preparatory Notes

The year was 2002, a cold November night, when taking a break from a friendly game of cards I got mixed up with a newspaper ... The North Texas Journal. Later, its name was changed to The Journal of North Texas, an appeasement to someone in the Panhandle with a publication going by the same name. Not knowing very much about the real reason for the name change, I just assumed the paper furthest to the north - the Panhandle being further north than the Red River Country would have first choice keeping the name. Made sense to me - did then, and still does. It is hardly remembered now as anything but the latter of the two names, The Journal of North Texas.

In the hall, just off the dining room, some of my photographs hung on a wall. They had been visible all evening from where we sat playing cards. Seldom do I print, matt, and frame one image. I like sets of two, three or five, never four, interrelated images, usually the same subject matter put together to form a story; often a study of the same subject matter from afar, closer, and close up. The photographs that hung on this wall were five images taken at the Albuquerque Balloon Festival. It was a blustery October morning as the hot air balloons were being inflated with propane generated air so they could begin the morning mass ascension into a cold, cloudy, sky.

Touring our home for the first time, playing cards left lying on the table, Tom and Kit Chase, especially Kit, editor at that time for the North Texas Journal, seemed to have an interest in these images. Other pictures hung here and there throughout the house. This set of five photographs, however, kept her still for more than a moment.

Kit was not coy when she asked if I would like to go up in the air and take pictures of a group of men who would parachute in the same manner as was done in World War II – low elevation, on a static line, from a twin propeller transport plane. No genuine fear of flying, I did not have to think it over. I just said yes. Kit then said I could write the story if I liked. I again told her yes, expressing to her an affinity for writing just as I have for making pictures.

A few weeks later I spent all Saturday at the Gainesville Municipal Airport. I mingled with the men of the WWII Airborne Demonstration Team and the many people who had come out to witness the low level jump. The difference would be my observations of the men making the jump would come from inside the C47 as opposed to watching from the ground.

Yes, that story is here between the covers. It is the epitome of present circumstances coupled with the past, manifesting itself as a state of mind called then and now.

The story was not expressly written as such at the time, but how else could it have been recorded? A group of men re-enacting something now that happened then, done in time period uniforms, flying in and jumping out of a plane of the type that was used during World War II and done so at and above the City of Gainesville airport. Possessing direct ties to the past, the airport was built by the United States Army in conjunction with the 59,000 acre Camp Howze, a World War II training camp.

I wrote some more articles and did some photo journalism before Kit moved on to another newspaper. I loved it! Not so long after Kit left the Journal of North Texas my idea of a column entitled Cooke County Then & Now became reality.

March 11, 2004, Cooke County Then & Now appeared for the first time in print. It was not the subject matter I had planned, but the timing was such that when a good friend asked that I do an article on the NOSCOGA Federal Credit Union, I told him sure. I switched gears and wrote my first Cooke County Then & Now column like that of an assignment about the great success of NOSCOGA. They were celebrating their 47th year in business. To my delight, the column was well received. It is the second chapter in this book. Ironically, it was a story with ties to that good friend that I had wanted to lead off with as my debut column. That story published on April 11th is the first chapter in this book.

That is how Cooke County Then & Now began. There would have been no column, however, were it not for certain events and circumstances.

Getting here, moving to Gainesville was one event.

Life in Gainesville began for us several years earlier.

Moving to Gainesville, Texas in 1999 was not like the travel and work I had left behind. Roughly for fifteen years we had moved from one town or one city to another. An assignment as a project superintendent, a project manager, or a resident engineer always seemed to be offered at or near the completion of a given project. Working my way out of a job here, hoping and somehow always winding up with another job there, the sign of doing my job.

Home was some abstract thing we flew or drove to when time allowed. Museum like, we cared for it inside and out and usually placed new objects within. Then, we would lock up and leave until the next visit.

The project locations were always in cities of good size - that is where the work usually is. Most of that work on the fringes of those colossal habitats of humanity - that is where cities usually grow, at their extremities.

This was different. I had made a conscious choice to accept a position at The University of North Texas in Denton. That choice, within the constraints of time, of distance, of money, was why we chose where we would live.

Gainesville, in the glow of a setting evening sun draws a soul in. Just beyond the fast food eateries, the quick stop inconvenience stores, and the roar of Interstate 35, California Street is alluring. Black light posts with large white archaic looking lights cast a soft and inviting light on the sidewalks and storefronts along each side of California Street. Side streets jutting north or south of California Street are paved in red brick. Unique old buildings of the past on both sides of the streets of Historic Olde Towne Gainesville stand as silent reminders of the past. It is charming. The weary traveler might just choose to stay if only because it is a welcome sight looking east up California Street as far as the eye can see.

The choice to make Gainesville our home was not too surprising. Our former residence was in Bisbee. A small mining town in southeastern Arizona. It was once a tough and colorful, wild at times, bustling town of thousands. The past does not just linger there, but is everywhere. From boom to bust it is much like Gainesville. In Bisbee it was the mining of copper, silver, and gold that brought the people there. In Gainesville it was the land, farming, ranching and oil. Both have survived the past.

Opening a bookstore was another event creating special circumstances.

Two years after moving to Gainesville, we opened Lone Star Book Scouters. Two years later we moved the store from the 113 N. Commerce location into the old Watts Brothers Pharmacy at 103 South Commerce.

What was Lone Star Book Scouters now became StarrBooks. Have you ever written a check out to Lone Star Book Scouters? Try answering the phone, it is a long name to write, a mouthful to enunciate. The move to another location made it easy to shorten the name and do a play on words. The Star derived from the original name, the added r in the Starr done to honor one of my wife's Cherokee ancestors, add books and you have StarrBooks.

Sometimes people confuse our well known bookstore with that coffee shop that goes by a similar name. People have mistakenly gone there first looking for a good book, but finding only good coffee. Conversely, someone might happen into our store looking for a good cup of coffee, finding to their surprise a good book and a good cup of coffee served from behind the counter of the olde fashioned soda fountain still in operation inside StarrBooks. It was never the intent to cause any confusion for the good coffee people from the Northwest. We really do not mind the mixup, and they probably appreciate our help in making their name well known in these parts.

I'll admit being referred to as an outsider the first time I was caught off guard. I don't know why? I had to consider exactly what that meant.

In our travels from one place to another, working the ephemeral construction jobs, we were never anything but. I suppose though in the motels, the RV Parks, the apartments, everyone was. We went unnoticed. In the business, those individuals we worked with never seemed to take issue with who we were, where we came from, or how long we would be there. Then perhaps they had it figured for what it was - the work would be done, the job would end, and most of us would be on our way out of town. How true.

The second time I was referred to as an outsider, I thought briefly of the bumper sticker that reads, "I wasn't born in Texas, but I got here as quick as I could." I looked that person in the eye and stated with wild enthusiasm and a bit of cockiness, "I wasn't born here, but I got to Gainesville as quick as I could."

There are probably some who still do, will always consider us, and many like us, to be outsiders. Yet to many, those who have touched our lives, we never were. In their eyes and minds we have fit right in.

What does moving here, opening a bookstore, and being an outsider have to do with the column Cooke County Then & Now? Everything! It is a perfect blend of events having created circumstances that would cause any person to develop a great desire to learn more about and share Gainesville and Cooke County's rich and varied history. Living here and owning a bookstore adds up. Being the outsider part of the equation might not seem congruous with writing a column about Cooke County and Gainesville. Consider this ...

I am originally from Arizona. Arizona is diverse in its geography and within its borders are some phenominal natural wonders. Its history deep, rich, and colorful, and there is plenty to see and do there. So why did I not write a column about Tucson, or Page, or Sierra Vista? Most of us do not appreciate the uniqueness, the rich history, the heritage of the place where we were born and raised. The Grand Canyon, it's just another big canyon right? A Painted Desert - why would anybody go out into the desert to paint? Geronimo, another mean and tough Indian? Who was Father Kino, did I go to school with his son? All very common banalities to one who grew up in Arizona.

Transplanted, the fascination of where we end up; the people, it's origin, the time line in what made it what it is today, are so very interesting to the outsider. All that is new and different is almost mesmerizing when first delving into it. Cooke County Then & Now gave me the opportunity to talk to interesting people of the area, research the various subjects I wrote about, and learn while I wrote.

Now that I have been away from Arizona for so many years I find myself reading more and more about the place where I grew up. Learning, imagining, and frankly wishing sometimes I were there again. I'll bet some outsider is writing about my town, my Tucson, in the Arizona Highways I receive each month. Oh, the irony!

So many good people have come through the doors of StarrBooks right from the beginning. I have learned much about Gainesville and Cooke County because of the store. Opportunities for the choosing have come and gone. Cooke County Then & Now would never have become an idea, much less a reality were it not for the people of Gainesville and Cooke County.

There was quite an array of people and subject matter that in one form or another begged to be written. Some were floating ideas of the mind. A few were underway as scribbled notes, an outline, a first draft. Others were just ideations coming directly or indirectly from people that had visited with me somewhere along the way, in the store, out and about. Several of the columns that appear in this book were never published.

Most intriguing, most compelling to write of is the story of rumored, lost buried treasure in Cooke County. How, where, and when I could not begin to tell even if I wanted. A crusty old man who wandered into the bookstore one day with the story never did return to elaborate on the small morsels of information he left behind. I can still smell the slow simmering stew, but will never get to taste of it. It was, he told me, his great, great grandfather who had somehow been involved in a robbery in which a large sum of money had been taken, including quite a lot of gold coins. Buried, he went on, along the banks of the Red River, never recovered by the robbers nor anyone else. He was to contact me so we might find a time and place to 'have a smoke and sip a little whiskey' while he would orate his tale. Who was he? Why did he not return? Perhaps I was too eager and asked too many questions. Maybe he died.

Tom Binford allowed me to interview him. I am sorry I did not complete that column. There was an old house that was to be remodeled and I would follow it's transformation from the old to the new while telling of its inhabitants then and now. Rosston and what might have come of a visit there still sticks in my mind. Camp Howze was to be the backdrop for many more columns. Author, June Rayfield Welch was to be central to a column about his book *Dave's Tune*. The oldest house in Cooke County, tornados, Pete Briscoe's store, Levines - the list long and varied, those connections of then to now I wished to make.

The year was 2004, and on January 13th the last issue of The Journal of North Texas was published. The thoughts of what to write for the next issue ceased to be necessary. The hurriedness to get the final draft corrected, text, and pictures sent to Charles no longer occupied any place or time in my life. Picking up a copy of the paper to read was no longer possible. The Journal of North Texas and the column Cooke County Then & Now quietly gave way to becoming a thing of the past.

There could not have been a book were it not for a few good people aside from the many who contributed with images, material, and ideas. Kit Chase who opened a door for me. Charles Huddleston who published my photographs, stories, and the column Cooke County Then & Now. Bill Riley who is not just a deep well of story ideas and information, but who is an inspiration and a good friend. Bill never treated me as an outsider, he from the day we met always made me feel as though I belonged. Louis Stephenson, the person who keeps the humor of our days in Gainesville in proper proportion through thick and thin.   No book can be left untouched without some good editing.   My editor never gave up no matter how much I screamed, kicked, and yelled while she sat at the keyboard making corrections and small changes. Thank you Kathie.

Please enjoy the book Cooke County Then & Now.

Timothy
August 2006
Gainesville, Texas

The north side of the square in 1914 from Commerce Street
on the west to Dixon Street on the east.
Courtesy of StarrBooks

In 2006 the north side of the square is not all visible from about
the same spot the 1914 image was taken. From right to left businesses
in the block are Gene's Photo, Bella Matiz, Anjanette's Chocolate and
Truffle Shoppe, Vines and Branches, and Memory Lane Antique Mall.

© 2004 Timothy L. Parks

"They camped near Black Hill out there, directly behind my house. Near the highest point of the hill I would think, but I don't really know where exactly they camped," Bill said. "Out there somewhere," he pointed in the general vicinity.

Kiowa Indian Raid of 1868

The year was 1868. I don't suppose there is anybody still around who recalls first hand a certain event that occurred early in the winter of that year. No of course not. But there are those who remember it from the telling and retelling of it, and by reading about it. And there are those who think about it often, perhaps every day. Bill Riley is one of those who does just that.

Inviting me out to his place last summer, I drove the mile or so west of Leonard Park to College View Subdivision, then pulled into a nicely shaded drive on College View. It was hot, the shade of a large leafy tree a welcome relief making the heat a little tolerable.

Bill walked out and met me there at my vehicle, then motioned that we should walk around to the back of his place. Behind the house we stopped. Just as I began to look out and survey the land to the east, Bill ducked down in front of me and exclaimed, Whew!

Ducking down myself I quickly looked around and said, "Whew what?"

"Well, I just missed that arrow."

"What arrow? What are you talking about?"

"Why I'm livin' here where those Indians camped that night, so I just barely missed an arrow ... oh by about a hundred and thirty five and a half years," he mused.

Bill moved here in 1965. Although a subdivision now, the area then was open with few houses and people. The rise and high point of the land is called Black's Hill.

Recorded in history, back in January of 1868, the last Indian raid of major consequence in Cooke County was staged by a band of Kiowa Indians numbering between 100 to 200 - the exact number will never be known, it varies depending upon what account you go by. They were led by a young chief named Big Tree. Working east, from the northwestern part of the county, the Indians rustled horses, pillaged and plundered , scalped and killed all the way to Gainesville.

It was here on the east side of Elm Creek, below what was at that time the Samuel Doss place, that the first long day of the two day foray of January 5th and 6th concluded. "They camped near Black Hill out there, directly behind my house. Near the highest point of the hill I would think, but I don't really know where exactly they camped," Bill said. "Out there somewhere," he pointed in the general vicinity.

Twice a day, every day since retiring Bill walks. Once in the morning and then again in the evening, a regimented routine that he seldom misses unless he is out of town. Up until his retirement his walks were never, could never be that frequent, but he made the walk when he could.   His route has always been the same: From behind his home he ambles east, northeast across the clearing headed for the thick trees that line the hills and embankment of Elm Creek.   Into the thick, green growth he disappears and makes the trek down towards Elm Creek and then back up again.

Bill led me across the flat grassy area and we disappeared from view into the trees. Of his countless walks down this trail Bill speaks of a few unusual occurrences. "I couldn't tell you when they each happened, it's been awhile back. Once, just past this old burnt-down house, as I walked down the trail a horse-apple just fell out of the tree. It didn't hit me, just fell right beside me. I stopped and looked around - saw nothing or nobody. To this day I don't know where it came from or how it might've come to fall right in my path. It kind of raised the hair on the back of my neck." Through a thin smile Bill said, "There are no horse-apple trees you know."

The Indian foray had begun west of Gainesville, in the Willa Walla Valley of eastern Montague County, they then crossed over into Cooke County near the headwaters of Clear Creek. Before making camp Sunday evening, seventeen miles to the east near Black's Hill above Elm Creek, they had killed nine people.   Under a dark, cold and stormy night - a blue norther had blown in - a group Indians that for whatever reason had split off from the main party, came into town from the north, on the east side of Elm Creek. They entered Gainesville seemingly without knowing it. Alarmed at finding themselves in town, they departed quickly leaving behind a couple of horses and other effects, reuniting with the main Kiowa party encamped on the other side of the Elm Creek. The people of Gainesville had slept through the short, uninvited visitation.

Sometime before daybreak the Indian encampment broke and they hastily departed the area possibly because they feared being discovered, but more likely because they had been caught unawares when the temperatures plummeted and the freezing sleet and snow began to fall. They made their way west, the same way they had come the day before, but not without killing and taking more hostages. In all thirteen people were killed before Big Tree and his Kiowa raiding party left Cooke County for good sometime during the day, January 6, 1868.

On another trek along the trail down to Elm Creek, not too much farther down the trail from where that horse-apple fell, a big old branch just dropped right in his path, didn't hit him, but stopped Bill right in his tracks. A branch better explained than a horse-apple, yet his hair still raised off the back of his neck. I could feel my hair raising too, becoming charged at the exciting notion of unexplained events.

Finally, Bill tells of one afternoon as he headed down the trail with his two dogs. The big one, a black Labrador Retriever named Sambo just stopped and acted like something was wrong - didn't bark, didn't fuss, just stood there. The little mixed breed, Queenie, did the same only she went down on here belly, feet out in front of her. "So I did too," said Bill, "I stopped in my tracks that is, I didn't ly down on my belly. We sort of just hung there in limbo for a moment - a long moment - and then all of a sudden the little dog yapped, jumped up and broke the spell, and that was that."

About the odd occurrences, Bill didn't offer up any

explanations, but calmly said, "Sometimes I just wonder about those times out there on the trail."

As we strode back up the hard packed pathway and broke out into bright sunlight I considered the wild band of Kiowa Indians that had camped here on this land one night, a long time ago.   One night out of how many times the sun has risen and set on Black's Hill since then? Before then? What else has happened here that nobody now lives to tell about?

A view of an area below Black Hill, one possible
location of the Kiowa Indian camp.

Between tree branches, the Cooke County Courthouse can be seen.
Below it is about where Bill's trail heads down to Elm Creek.

NASCOGA

The old National Supply office complex as it sits today on the west
side of Interstate 35, just north of Gainesville proper. The low roof
structure in the forefront the former office complex.
Courtesy of NASCOGA

NASCOGA

The year was 1956. Do you remember when NASCOGA Credit Union opened its door for business? Few people would probably recall the quiet event that took place on May 15th of that year. Through a single door into a small office tucked away in the back of the National Supply Company office complex, NASCOGA Credit Union was chartered and opened for business. (NASCOGA is the acronym for National Supply Company Gainesville) There were, that first day of business, ten charter members and assets slightly in excess of $25.00. Business was conducted for just a few short hours each day, and all services were performed voluntarily by members. Today members are counted in the thousands and as of December 31, 2003 assets totaled $27,096,969.

National Supply Plant came to Gainesville in 1954 to manufacture steel products for the oil industry. With plants all over the country, the Gainesville plant would become the 11th to open. Mr. Heywood, the plant manager, and Mr. Hyde, the personnel manager, were the first two men to arrive in town. The plant was located on the west side of Interstate 35 just north of Gainesville proper. Peter Hyde was aware that the other plants all had credit unions, and knew of their success - he went to work early in 1955 to get a credit union started for this plant. It was a federal credit union examiner, Addison C. Head, who assisted Peter in the process of doing what was necessary to get his idea off the ground.

Joe Wilson was the first member of NASCOGA. Just lately Joe was reminiscing. He commented on the matter of getting a loan: "In the early days of the credit union they could approve a loan easily, but couldn't make a loan until they got somebody to come in and deposit some money to cover the loan." For the first three years, as membership grew and assets increased, daily business was run totally by volunteers until 1959 when Marge Brown came to work becoming the first paid full-time employee of NASCOGA.

Extremely loyal and dedicated, the growing membership and amount of business activity became such that the space required to take care of credit union business in the former security guard office would no longer suffice; consequently a new home had to found. From the small back room location at the plant office building, NASCOGA moved to Plaza 82 in 1976. Assets at that time totaled 1 million dollars, the oil industry was booming and National Supply had by then become the largest employer in Cooke County.

In the fifties, as done in all financial institutions in that time period, all transactions were posted by hand. Amazingly, at NASCOGA, they were done that way until 1981. Membership then was 1700 and there was 3 million dollars assets. The task quite formidable in consideration of the fact there were at that time only two full-time paid employees. Imagine that!   Evelyn Otto was one of those two, she had come to work in 1979 as a fill in and never left. It was then the Board of Directors contacted EDS (Electronic Data Systems) and soon thereafter all member transactions and payroll deductions were computerized. The general ledger, however, was not. It would be another nine years before it too went the way of the computer. Whew, what a relief!

When layoffs began at National Supply in 1982, and in 1983 the number of employees had dwindled to 250, the NASCOGA membership declined and the number of delinquencies increased. Evelyn became the manager in 1982 replacing Patty Wallace and remembers well when Federal examiners suggested that NASCOGA become a community credit union or expand by taking in new companies. Done so hesitantly, the Board of Directors decided to take in other companies - the first to be invited was Poly Pipe. They accepted the invitation. By 1987 NASCOGA had become a diversified group of companies including such familiar names as Scivally's, Joe Walter Lumber Company, Unimax Hearing Instruments, North American Orthodontic Lab, Anderson Trailer Company.

Just how and why did NASCOGA Federal Credit survive the demise of National Supply, the very company it was sponsored by? Evelyn Otto knows a good part of the reason.. She says "Even though the plant was closing and the workers being let go it was amazing the fierce loyalty our members had. I mean, just because they were no longer working for National Supply, had to go out and get different jobs with different companies ... I'd say

90% of them stayed on with the credit union and kept their accounts, kept doing business." Even labor and management, notorious for not always being like minded on a lot of workplace issues, left that distinction and their differences outside the door. All the employees felt a pride of ownership and were each equal in their participation.

The NASCOGA Credit Union of then has not just survived, but has thrived and become the NASCOGA Federal Credit Union as it is now known. Since 1996 they have done business from a newly built facility on Lawrence Street just south of Highway 82. In 1998 NASCOGA was awarded approval by the National Credit Union Association (NCUA) for a community charter allowing service to the people who live, work or attend school in Cooke County. There are plans for an expansion, for satellite offices, for additional services. Just as it was then, the seven member board of directors are elected, serve a two year term and do so voluntarily as do the three members of the credit committee. And just as it was when they began, older members, and new ones alike, remain and are to steadfast in their loyalty to NASCOGA.

Writers Note:

Evelyn Otto retired in 1997 from her manager position, Debbie Endres took here place. Present volunteer board members serving now are: Kenneth Hermes, Lynn Stiles, JoAnne Prestage, Will Bezner, Greg Zimmerer, Phil Newton and Pam Hoedebeck. Serving on the credit committee are Jack Dyer, Marcia Porter and M.C. Legge. The list of companies whose employees are able to join and benefit from NASCOGA Federal Credit Union number 29 at last count.

Plaza 82 where NASCOGA moved to from it original location in the
National Supply office complex. This view the north elevation
and sign as seen from Highway 82.

© 2004 Timothy L. Parks

NASCOGA Federal Credit Union as looks today
at its Lawrence Street location.

© 2004 Timothy L. Parks

A Great American

Early in 1951, Marine recruits prepare to leave Gainesville by bus.
From left to right are Jack "JD" Wages, Georga "Bosa" Davis,
Wally Johnson, Paul Townsend, Marine Recruiter, and Richard Helm,.
Prepared as usual, Wally had a suitcase, whereas,
all the others had a small bag.

A Great American

The year was 1950 and on June 25th North Korea invaded South Korea. At the UN's request, and only two days later, President Truman ordered U.S. Forces into Korea. The Korean War was underway.

One year earlier, in a junior year Gainesville High School English class, an essay assignment was given. A take off on a Readers Digest feature, the teacher had instructed each student in the class to write about "My Favorite Character", that one person in class who best fit the title, whomever that favorite character might be. When all the essays were handed in, and the teacher began to go through them, it became obvious the class had viewed the assignment as more of an election; rather than the creative process of writing and describing one's favorite character. After all the votes had been counted by the teacher, Wallace Johnson had won by a landslide. In fact, all 30-some members of the class had written about him.

Grading the papers for the teacher was easy - they all received an "F" and the papers were torn up; the notion rejected by one person that any one person could be everybody's favorite character. Each student was then dictatorially instructed to try it again, this time Wally would not be the subject.

In school and out, Wally was always cutting up. He and a friend once climbed to the top of the dome of the old high school building and painted it. He didn't get in trouble for that. Oh yes, they got caught, but the colors they chose to use were, after all, the school colors. Bored in class, it was not uncommon for Wally to climb out of a window and take off, the other kids covering for him.

He was a football player, a good one at that. Tom Woods, one of Wally life long friends, said of him, "He was the fastest fullback I've ever seen."

Weekends, Wally and his friends would often cross the Red River and frequent some of the bars there in Thackerville, Oklahoma. Too young to drink, Sheriff Ladell would pick them up, bring then back across the river into Texas and tell them not to come back to Love County.

Even then, Wally thought and lived independently. He laughed at life and made people laugh. He was fair and honest, hated bullies and always took up for the underdog. Wally was perhaps like that of some situation comedy television character acting out his part each and every day. He enjoyed his high school days.

Late in 1950 of their senior year, without having finished High School, a number of young men from Gainesville High School enlisted in the United States Marine Corp so that they might be trained and serve their country fighting in the Korean War. Wallace Johnson was one of them.

There were five young men who went to Sherman

to sign on: Jack "JD" Wages, Georga "Bosa" Davis, Wally Johnson, Paul Townsend and Richard Helm. "Of these guys," tells Regean Vestal, "All of them but Jack were going to join the Navy; Jack was there to enlist in the Marines. They got to Sherman and the Navy recruiter was gone, he was closed that day. So, the rest of them said, we might as well join the marines too - we're here."

They all went to Korea.

The Korean War did not end until Armistice was signed July 27, 1953. Killed in battle during the Korean War were 33,652 American servicemen and women. Injured were 103,284. Wallace Johnson was among the injured. His tour of duty short; for he was shot, suffered an extremely serious head injury in a fierce, major battle. For his service he was decorated with several Purple Hearts and a Bronze Star!

Throughout his life Wally remained independent in his thinking and actions. He watched out for the good of people, sought after justice, and was looked up to by his peers in all that he pursued in life. He pursued much. He never quit joking. Mikki Jones, owner of Bella Matiz, said, "Wally was ornery, oh my gosh he was. But he was tasteful when he was, he was very tasteful. He could say the funniest things. You never knew at times if he was serious or not."

Wally's last fight was against Lou Gehrig's disease. "He took it with dignity. I never heard a word of complaint, nor did anybody else. He never said why me God one time," Nita, his beloved wife recalls. "He fought it the best he could and joked to the very end."

When it was time to leave this dying world and begin a life everlasting he went peacefully. Surrounded by many of his friends his last words were, "Tell everybody that I love em', and stay sober." Wallace Johnson was a "Great American" - he died October 8, 2002.

Writer's Note:

Given an assignment to write about "My Favorite Character", if we had known Wallace Johnson then or now, I think we would all have written about him too. Thank you Nita Johnson, Reagan Vestal, Micky Jones and Tom Woods for sharing.

Wally Johnson
Courtesy of Nita Johnson

Wally Johnson

Courtesy of Nita Johnson

Military Bugler
Courtesy Photograph

Taps

The year was 1862, during the Civil War, Union Army Captain Robert Ellicombe was with his men near Harrison's Landing in Virginia. The Confederate Army was on the other side of the narrow strip of land.

Late, one of those quiet, dark nights after doing battle, Captain Ellicombe could hear the moans of a soldier who lay wounded on the battlefield. Deciding to risk his life, whether he be of the Union Army or the Confederate Army, he ventured out into the field, crawling on his belly to avoid gun fire and brought back the stricken soldier for medical attention. Upon returning to his encampment the Captain found his effort had been in vain, the soldier who he knew now was a Confederate, had died.

In the light of a dim lantern, he looked down upon the dead man, his breath became short as he went into a stupor. The face of the soldier he looked into was that of his own son. Studying music in the South when the war broke out, not letting his father know, he had enlisted in the Confederate Army. Now he lay dead for the cause of the Confederacy.

Heartbroken, Captain Ellicombe asked permission of his superiors to give his son a full military burial despite his enemy status. The request was denied. The Captain then asked if he could have a group of Army band members play a funeral dirge for his son. That request was also denied. Out of respect for the father, a Captain, they did allow one musician at the burial.

Choosing a bugler, he asked the bugler to play a small musical score he had found among the few personal items taken from his dead son's uniform.

What this lonely bugler played is the touching, yet haunting and mournful melody we now know as Taps.

The story as told above, or any other version of it found elsewhere, unfortunately is said to be a myth.

The true story recorded, tells of Brigadier General Daniel Butterfield, being responsible for Taps. The General disliked the banal "Extinguish Lights" bugle call then in use. He summoned one evening to his tent Brigade Bugler, Private Oliver Wilcox Norton. He supposedly whistled a new tune asking that Private Norton sound it out. When finally the general became satisfied with one of the many spontaneous and repeated tries, an arrangement that met with the general's approval was used that night.

Years later Oliver Wilcox Norton was quoted as saying ...

"One day in July 1862, the Army of the Potomac was in camp at Harrison's Landing on the James River resting and recruiting from its losses in the seven days of battle before Richmond, Virginia. General Butterfield summoned the writer to his tent, and whistling some tune, asked the bugler to sound it for him. This was done, not quite to his satisfaction at first, but after repeated trials, changing the time of some of the notes, which were scribbled on the back of an envelope, the call was finally arranged to suit the General."

There are many bugle calls, but it is Taps that so many of us so readily recognize. Even as kids we mimicked the mournful sound by means other than that of a bugle.   Done so in play, we did it with reverence knowing well what those notes meant and mean today.

The words that go along with Taps are not so familiar and there are several variations. It is these words though that are most commonly thought of when the solitary bugler stands alone and plays.

Day is done, gone the sun,
From the hills, from the lake,
From the sky.
All is well, safely rest,
God is nigh.

Go to sleep, peaceful sleep,
May the soldier or sailor,
God keep.
On the land or the deep,
Safe in sleep.

Love, good night, Must thou go,
When the day, And the night
Need thee so?
All is well. Speedeth all
To their rest.

Fades the light; And afar
Goeth day, And the stars
Shineth bright,
Fare thee well; Day has gone,
Night is on.

Thanks and praise, For our days,
'Neath the sun, Neath the stars,
'Neath the sky,
As we go, This we know,
God is nigh.

From the invocation delivered by at the Taps Exhibit Opening Ceremony at Arlington National Cemetery, May 28,1999 Chaplain (Colonel) Edward Brogan (USAF, Ret.) Said ....

"Lord of our lives, our hope in death, we cannot listen to Taps without our souls stirring. Its plaintive notes are a prayer in music - of hope, of peace, of grief, of rest. Prepare us too, Lord, for our final bugle call when you summon us home! When the trumpet of the Lord shall sound and death will be no more."

Writers Note:

Of the two, I prefer to believe the myth which lends credence that a so enduring arrangement would come from a sad and mournful heart as opposed to disdain for a melody. Perhaps it was Brigadier General Daniel Butterfield who gave Captain Robert Ellicombe permission to have the lone bugler play at his sons burial?

Brigadier General Daniel Butterfield
Courtesy Photograph

Dr. Benjamin A. Bugg pictured here with his beard touching the floor
was featured in a Ripley's Believe It Or Not Column. The photograph
was taken in Nashville and thought to be the one used
by Ripley's.
Courtesy of Martha J. Liddell

Believe It Or Not

The year was 1874 when John Sanders Bugg and family moved to Gainesville. A few years after that, his brother, Dr. Benjamin A. Bugg, also moved here from Arkansas. In Arkansas, aside from being a doctor, Dr. B. A. Bugg had raised fine quarter horses. Members of the Bugg family were well known for the race horses they bred and raised.

But, before Arkansas and Texas, it was while living in Couchville, Tennessee that Dr. Benjamin A. Bugg was featured in a Ripley's Believe Or Not column for his long beard. It was not just the length that caught someone's attention, the fact that it swept the floor made it all the more unusual.

How long was his beard if measured from his chin to the floor, and then beyond that, the added length that would have it drag the floor if allowed to do so? How tall did Benjamin stand? From the photograph, using the step as a gauge - steps are usually about 7" in height - he was, relatively speaking, a tall man, likely close to 6' tall. His

beard then would have measured something less than 5 ½'
to have touched the floor and more if it was able to sweep
the floor.

The average beard grows 5 ½" a year. Let's just say
that Dr. Bugg's beard was 6' long. It would have taken 13
years for him to grow it, probably more as some trimming
must have taken place over that long span of time.

Benjamin was born in 1835. Before the Civil War he
was a resident of Couchville, Tennessee. Because he was a
doctor he was exempt from conscription and, therefore, did
not fight. Three of his brothers, however, - Jesse, James,
and John did. They fought for the Confederacy. Another
brother - William - fought for the Union. Pitting brother
against brother was not an uncommon contradiction of the
Civil War, but it is not believed that they ever faced off
from each other in battle. Jesse, James and John survived
the war, it is not known if William made it back or not.
John had been a prisoner - captured at Ft. Donaldson -
and later in the war found freedom by way of a prisoner
exchange.

In the Bugg family, there was one other brother,
Samuel Bugg; and one sister, her name was Tabatha.
William and Samuel were the only ones that did not come
to Texas.

Presently, the longest known beard on a living
male is recorded in the Guinness World Book of Records
belonging to Shamsher Singh of Punjab, India. It measures
6' from chin to tip. The longest beard ever grown was by
Hans Langseth of Norway. Upon his death in Kensett,
Iowa in 1927 it was measured to be 17' 6" inches long.
In 1967 it was presented to the Smithsonian Institute in
Washington D. C.

With age, Benjamin was no longer able to care for his long beard; he cut and shaved it off. Dr. B. A. Bugg died in 1910. At Fairview Cemetery, Dr. Benjamin A. Bugg rests peacefully in the Bugg family plot.

Writer's Note:

A special thanks to Martha J. Liddell for sharing about such an interesting member of her family. Dr. B. A. Bugg is her Great, Great, Great Uncle.

At the Bugg family plot Martha J. Liddell stands just to the right of
Dr. B. A. Bugg's headstone.
© 2004 Timothy L. Parks

JUG OF WHISKEY

From a scant few log homes built along Elm Creek in 1850,
Gainesville had grown significantly
in a short 30 years.
Courtesy of StarrBooks

General Edmund Pendleton Gaines
Courtesy of Mrs. Helen Ellerbe.

Jug of Whiskey

The year was 1847 when at a location some three miles, south and east of what is now Gainesville, a small log stockade began to take shape. Built to protect settlers from Indian forays, the small outpost was called Fort Fitzhugh. It was so named for Colonel William F. Fitzhugh, who had led a group of Texas Rangers who voluntarily came over from Collin County to construct the fort.

Fort Fitzhugh was chosen in 1850 to be the county seat of Cooke County. Renamed Liberty, Texas, its distinction as the county seat and its name were ephemeral. Liberty was found to have already been taken by another Texas township and to the northwest a small new settlement nestled near the banks of Elm Creek became the county seat instead.

I can no better state how the location of Gainesville was chosen that 15th day of August 1850 than to quote W.R. Strong just as A. Morton Smith did in his book *The First Hundred Years In Cooke County*.

In his memoirs, W.R. Strong said,

I have always been told the location of the town was decided this way: Uncle Bob Wheelock (chief justice) came up to the group of citizens standing in the proposed Wheeler Creek site while they were trying to decide. He picked up a jug of whiskey and said, 'All in favor of putting the town here, come with me,' and he proceeded to the Mary E. Clark site, which was finally approved.

Gainesville went dry in the year 1910 and did not allow the sale of alcohol again until just after the turn of another century. One would think instead of teetotaling for almost a hundred years there should have a been - should be - Whiskey Jug Days to celebrate and honor the founding of Gainesville. But that was 1850, and for all we know, they may have celebrated and drank many jugs of whiskey in the days, months and years after that date in August of 1850 when Gainesville was founded. Perhaps a little too much. Hence the reason the town went dry. Perhaps?

In naming the town situated on the forty acre tract donated by Mary E. Clark, it was Colonel William F. Fitzhugh who made the recommendation that the town might be named for and in honor of a General who had served most all his life in the United States Army.

Edmund Pendleton Gaines was born in Virginia in 1777. He first served in a local militia in North Carolina. From 1799 until sometime in 1807 he served in the United States Sixth Infantry, the Fourth Infantry, and the Second Infantry. It was while serving in the Second that he participated in the arrest of Aaron Burr. Shortly thereafter, on an extended absence from military service, he practiced law in the Mississippi Territory.

When the War of 1812 broke out, he returned to the army. For his victorious leadership during his assignments in that war, he was promoted to Brigadier General. For his leadership in defending Fort Erie and defeating a British force far greater than his own, on August 15, 1815, a promotion to Major General, thanks from The United States Congress, and a gold medal were all bestowed upon him. Gravely wounded in the fighting, General Gaines was assigned command of Military District Six - Louisiana, Mississippi and Tennessee making up that area. In 1817 General Gaines began a series of assignments concerning the Creeks and Seminole Indians making peace, trying to make peace, or fighting them. He did so until 1832 when he was again wounded.

His service up to this point in time easily served as a just cause to name a town in honor of this decorated and dedicated, valiant soldier. In fact, three towns were ultimately named after General Edmund Pendleton Gaines - Gainesville, Florida, Gainesville, Georgia, and Gainesville, Texas

Colonel William F. Fitzhugh did not call upon the citizens of this yet unnamed town to call it Gainesville because of General Gaines' efforts to make Cooke County safe from marauding Indians. He would have been, however, welcome relief had he come and fought the Kiowa Indians.   Rather, it was the unofficial support and sympathy shown for the Texas Revolution and Sam Houston's Army and his army that made his name a permanent part of this Great State of Texas.

At the time of the Texas Revolution, General Gaines commanded the Southwest Military Division. Under orders, he posted the Sixth Infantry at Fort Jessup, Louisiana to prevent any participation by United States citizens in the revolution. However, should the sovereignty of the United States border be violated he could order it defended. Or, if any Indian uprisings occurred he could cross the border and quell them. It was Indian depredations that allowed General Gaines to assist Sam Houston and his army.

Under the orders of General Gaines, at times, many companies of soldiers were advanced across the border into east Texas to fend off Indians and sometimes Mexican soldiers who had sided together with the Indians to fight the Texans. Houston's Army was better able to deal with the Mexican invasion as a result of The United States Army quashing these Indian threats.

Did President Andrew Jackson assure Sam Houston the help of General Gaines and his Army if certain events occurred? It has been written there is proof he did. But, for over stepping his authority a number of times in dealing with the complexities the nearby Texas Revolution, he was ultimately removed from command and court-martialed. Against those charges of insubordination, he defended himself ... and was successful in having them dismissed. General Gaines continued to serve his country commanding the entire Eastern Division of the United States Army and finally was assigned command of the Western Division in January of 1849.

Cooke County was formed in 1849 and in June of that same year General Edmund Pendleton Gaines died. In 1850 a small town was named Gainesville on the suggestion by one who had served under him knowing well the greatness and integrity this man who except by birth just as well had been a Texan.

Writers Note:
  References: <u>The Handbook of Texas Online</u> and <u>The First Hundred Years In Cooke County</u> by A. Morton Smith

Fish Creek Lodge

Fish Creek Lodge at Marysville

Fish Creek Lodge

It was early in the 1860's when some land that ly on either side of Fish Creek began to be settled. In that area, some twenty some miles to the north and west of Gainesville, the town that sprang up there became known as Marysville. It was a town built upon the farming and ranching that surrounded it. To encourage business to move in, anyone who purchased a residential lot was given a business lot. By 1900 there were roughly 350 inhabitants of Marysville.

Just recently I was taken out to Marysville to see the Masonic Lodge that was built in 1892 that still stands today, and to meet ands speak with some of the lodge members. The lodge originally built in 1872 burnt. We - Bill Riley and I - left Gainesville allowing for enough time to arrive at the lodge, tour it, talk to some of the members and then to be gone before their meeting began.

Not unlike many small communities in the Republic of Texas, a Masonic Lodge was built in Marysville. The Ancient Free and Accepted Masons of Texas chartered

Fish Creek Lodge No. 344 in 1872. The lodge, aside from being the meeting place for Masons, like so many others was by plan and design built to serve as a schoolroom for the children of the community. Lodges were built two stories tall. The lower floor intended for use as a school room and the upper floor the meeting room for the Masons. In addition to the space provided for schooling, in many cases all or part of the teachers salary were funded by the lodge.

We were a bit early and Worshipful Master Jim Harris who would take us on a tour of the lodge was not there yet. C. G. Reeves was though. He comes in early to make the coffee, sort of set the tone for the monthly meeting. Does so every week. He is from Ozark Arkansas and has been a member of the Fish Creek Lodge since 1985. The aroma of the coffee was good.

When Jim did arrive he was quick to extend a friendly welcome. He has been a member here for about fifteen years. Not very long he tells me. Before retiring Jim worked for an international oil field service company in paces like Saudi Arabia, Libya, Argentina, Canada, the Arctic. He did directional (boring) work.

"What I like about this lodge", begins Jim, "Is that this is one of the original lodge buildings, the way Texas Masonry was set up. It was a small community, they all met by the light of the moon - which this is a "moon lodge" - and the reason for that so you could see to come and go. On Saturday evening all your farming towns - and they all were Saturday towns - everybody went to town on Saturday evening. Long about dusk they would ease off and go up to the lodge room."

"Will we have a full moon tonight?" I asked.

"No, it will be June the 2nd."

"But we'll have a moon tonight."

"Well hopefully!"

It was cloudy, a stiff breeze blowing out of the south, southwest.

"I hope so. Bill was telling me one he got lost making his way back in the dark. It might be nice to have some moonlight to see where the heck were going."

"Yea Jim", said Bill, One night I was out here for a meeting, it was wintertime and kind of overcast and I was going to take the back roads home. I drove about thirty minutes and all of a sudden I came right back by this building."

We all laughed at the thought of such a thing.

"These two story lodges were for the education program in Texas. I just feel like since we still a few of them left in Texas, I'd like to see them preserved as long as we can keep them going"

"I agree. Whether you're a member of the lodge or not it's a part of the history of the this state."

"Well, and it's a part of the history of Masonry."

These days, aside from the lodge and the Baptist Church that once had congregation of 200 souls, there is little else standing that would constitute what was once a thriving small town. The first floor of the lodge is a community center, no longer a school room. It was the depression that caused people to begin to leave the area, shrinking the town, it was World War Two, Camp Howze that all but did away with it when they bought up so much of the land around Marysville.

Times have changed and the days of one room school houses are a thing of the past. The Masons are still very much, however, involved the quality and continuation of educating our youth. Mirabeau B. Lamar , a Freemason who also served as the second President of the Republic of Texas was quoted years ago as saying: "The cultivated mind is the guardian genius of democracy" That motto was adopted by the University of Texas - it personifies how the Masons still regard education today.

"Cooke County is very fortunate," said Jim. "We have five lodges. We're a pretty close knit group here. I'll attend meetings at Era or Gainesville, sometimes over to Myra, sometimes down to Burns City. And of course Fish Creek. From the other four lodges members attend our meetings. There are only four Lodge members that live in the area, all the others come from the other lodges - they have duel memberships. C. G Reeves, Paul Goin, Duane Binford and Don Moon live in the area. You can have as many memberships as you can afford to pay for. And there are some who do belong to all five lodges in Cooke County."

Other that the structure itself there is not much left that is original.

"That bell there", Jim pointed, "Was originally up in the bell tower. And like so many old structures this one too bows in the middle caused by the settling of the foundation around the perimeter."

Jim went around opening up the windows on the north and on the south allowing a breeze to cut across the expanse of the meeting room. It felt pretty good for when we first came up the stairs into the room it was stuffy, hot, humid.

Bill told of time when some of the lodge members wanted to install air conditioning. Others in the lodge questioned doing so, expressing that they had never had it before, so why do we need it now.

Of the members opposing air conditioning Jim said, "One of the more outspoken on the matter was Tom Binford." Tom is today one of the oldest members of the lodge.

"Was it installed?"

"Oh yes", said Jim, "That was about six or seven years ago."

"Did you over rule Tom and the few others? I asked.

"No, we just put it in."

"How does Tom feel about it now?"

"He never has said. I'm not sure he realized we went ahead and did it."

Things in the old Fish Creek lodge building change, but it stands strong, just as it was built in 1892. It and the land it is situated in are calming and alluring to the passing strangers eye.

Writers Note:
Many thanks to Jim Harris and all of the Lodge members I was so fortunate to meet.

Jim Harris sits beside the bell that once rang in the tower above.
© 2004 Timothy L. Parks

A few of the members take a moment so a picture could be made.
In the back, form left to right are Jame Lane and B. J. Huller.
In the front from left to right are John Fletcher, Wallace
Stephenson, Bill Riley, C. G. Reed, Jim Harris, and Terry Farqhar.

Lucy Bradley Junkin in early 1920's
Courtesy of Betty Junkin Guest

The Woman of Tomorrow

The year was 1918 and it was May 24th when at Newsome Dougherty Memorial High School Lucy Bradley delivered her Graduation Address.

Was the message prophetic? Was this young writer a prodigy? Was she a visionary, perhaps born before her time? Possibly she possessed all of these traits.

Then, the address may have sounded like science fiction. Since science fiction is to some extent nothing more than hope and desire for change in the future, her address not unlike say that of the master, Robert Heinlein - a fair portion of what he wrote has come to pass.

I offer to you Lucy Bradley's *The Woman of Tomorrow*.

One beautiful Sunday morning in the early fifties, somewhere in New York, the congregation of a certain church was stirred to very keen excitement. A woman who actually admitted that she intended to practice medicine had dared to enter their midst. We may picture for ourselves the scene as Elizabeth Blackwell entered the door and advanced down the aisle. All eyes were fastened on the new comer. The women, their cheeks brimming with shame, drew their skirts closer as she passed; their excitement caused the flowers on their bonnets to tremble. The men, with pained expressions on their faces, drew back and wondered what action should be taken.

We smile today as the picture passes before us, but to those dear old-fashioned people it was a serious question indeed and deserved careful consideration. During those years women begged for, worked for, and, in some instances, fought for equal rights with men. When we pass from that picture and consider the women of today and their relation to men, we are astounded that so great change has been effected in so few years.

At last men, the rulers of this world of ours, are beginning to see that this demand is not only just but natural. Necessity has obliterated many time-honored customs and regulations. When the halls of the great universities began to become vacant, it was suggested that perhaps women might help to carry on higher education. Men have been forced to admit, though reluctantly, that women have not fallen below the high standards which many years have established. Women professors, women physicians and women lawyers have come from the universities and are succeeding wherever they are sent.

Once there were two ways open to woman: she might love, honor, and obey a man or she might remain single to be classed as a burden on her near relatives. Today the various channels that lie before any young woman cannot be counted. Along with other things, women have already in many states received the most treasured privilege of a democratic country -- the right to vote. Shall we not consider that the greatest step possible in women's advancement?

We have pictured the woman of the past; we have considered the woman of the present; but what of the woman of tomorrow? What the picture holds no one knows, but that many changes will take place is evident.

In the past, a woman's sphere differed from that of a man's. Her thoughts were not the same as his; her interests lay in a different channel and were widely separated from his. But with the dawn of the new day we shall find man and woman in all things united. Alike? No vastly different. But man will appreciate the woman's interests, and she will strive that his desires may be realized ... "the woman's cause is man's; they rise or sink together, dwarfed or god-like, bound or free."

Indeed the woman's mind has been fed a little knowledge; and as we all know, a little knowledge is a dangerous thing. The capable mind being fed little craves for more. The mothers of tomorrow's sons will be strong in body, mind and soul; and the sons themselves, therefore, will be stronger, mightier, better men than this world has ever owned.

The argument that woman's place is primarily in the home will always stand true. No system of laws nor change of conditions may turn the way of nature. But a home where the mother is interested in the welfare of her country, the education of her children and the betterment of her neighbors will be a happier home than where the mother is not interested in the conditions surrounding her.

If then the woman of tomorrow will be a better mother, a more interesting companion, and a truer citizen, why do people stand with distressed countenances and with hands uplifted in horror whenever the future woman is mentioned? It is impossible to picture in full the woman of tomorrow and the change she will make in this world. I can not believe that she will be more masculine than the woman of today. But her sphere will be widened, her influence will be extended, and through her work the world will be in greater harmony than ever before.

Writers Note:

I thank Betty Junkin Guest for her time and trouble in sending me this to read and enjoy. I most certainly did! Then she allowed me to reprint it here, and for that we can all be grateful. Precious and timeless, the voice of her mother lives on for those that will listen. Lucy Bradley Junkin was born in Gainesville 1903, she died in 1987.

Newsome Dougherty Memorial High School.
Courtesy of StarrBooks

Outfitted with all the gear of a World War II Paratropper, there is
only one way to wait to board the C47.

© 2002 Timothy L. Parks

Paratroopers Invade Airport

I am told: "You are about to ride on a sixty year old aircraft. It was built by young women who, just days before may have been just housewives. It was maintained by eighteen and nineteen year old mechanics and their nineteen and twenty year old supervisors under wartime conditions. If the aircraft goes up, we guarantee it will come down. That's all we guarantee." Mike went silent I said not a word and we both laughed a serious laugh. Michael Mike Zozula is the adjunct for the WWII Airborne Demonstration Team. As he handed me paperwork that would allow me to accompany the Airborne Demonstration Team on this flight and jump, Mike added. "There is always an element of risk."

I met another Michael, he is responsible for the packing of the parachutes and reserves, there is another rigger who is responsible for repairs. Mike, that's Michael Zozula, was in the 86th Airborne, he was a parachute rigger. About the jump he told me, "If I'm not the first one at the door I'll be the second one out. I carry a Browning automatic rifle and jump with it, that's why I have to be one of the first people out the door, because of that. I enjoy doing this a lot, I enjoy meeting a lot of the veterans and it really helps when you see a smile on their face."

A relationship between the two Michael's more than a good chance, this Mike is the son of Michael the adjunct.

I ran into Mike the adjunct not too long before boarding the aircraft. I said, "I met your son."

"Sorry." he said.

I repeated myself, "I met your son."

"Sorry", he stated again only this time looking straight at me grinning.

"Ah." I acknowledged his smile with my own, while thinking, son unlike father would be going up in the "Boogie Baby" to jump. I laughed to myself at the paperwork, self assured this man would not send his son, nor I for that matter, into a plane he was not certain would be coming down in a safe and respectable manner.

Prior to my being asked to get on the plane, I met Tom Mason. He is a veterinarian of large animals in Springtown, Texas. He joined the group about a year ago and is an army reservist in the 994th Medical Detachment out of Austin, Texas. Tom had this to say about the jump, "There's going to a lot of testosterone, adrenalin and cortisol. Cortisol is a stress hormone, so when you get stressed that's what makes you jumpy, of course then adrenalin will get your heart rate to blowing and going and testosterone is half the reason we do all this crazy stuff." I was feeling a bit jumpy and I was not even going to jump.

The aircraft had been empty for a spell save only the pilot Ray Cunningham, the copilot Paul Riser, WWII veteran Ralph Spina of the 506th Airborne, Richard Wolf acting as radioman and liaison between the pilot up in the flight deck and the Jump Master at the rear of the plane by the open door and myself.

This was no re-enactment for Ralph - he was there some sixty years ago. He jumped and fought in World War Two serving in the 506th Airborne Unit. HBO has done a special in on the 506th Airborne Unit. That special having won an Emmy and thereby taking Ralph to places he has not been before. He is quiet, and proud in a modest sort of way about his participation in the war and also about the HBO special and Emmy awards. Speaking of Tom Hanks and late author Stephen Ambrose, Ralph could not say enough good things about their relationship and the common ground they share regarding World War Two.

"What is your background?", I asked of Richard Wolf.

"Special Forces [Army], twenty four years. I'm retired. I served with a lot of World War Two and Korean veterans and have tremendous respect for them."

Richard Wolf is the man who actually founded the team. "Forming the team" he told me, "had been in planning stages for about twenty years prior to kicking it off it in 1995" Actually making that first jump in 1998 when this plane was located for use.

Then the order was given and The Airborne Demonstration Team began to board the aircraft, climbing slowly up the narrow three step aluminum ladder that is hung from the plane's deck edge. Richard Wolf reaches out and helps to pull each heavily laden paratrooper up into the plane as they appear at the door. First aboard was the Jump Master, Roger Wolf - no relation to Richard Wolf

- followed by each of the other fourteen men who would jump. The Jump Master by the way is the individual in command, the pilot taking direction from him.

The seats filled quickly, the men coming aboard filing to the front of the plane taking their seats on the long hard green benches on each side of the plane. There are depressions in the benches with an unlatched seat belt at where each man sits. The green large and round open ribbed construction, the size of the plane diminished as the benches on both sides of the aircraft were filled with paratroopers..

The pilot fired up one engine, the one on the left wing and shortly thereafter fired up the other on the right. We sat awhile before he began to taxi north to position the C47 for takeoff. On the taxi way at the end of the runway we sat some more before the engines could be are heard revving up.   Turning the plane ninety degrees and then ninety degrees more, the pilot lined up on the runway, opened up the throttle and we began to roll south down the runway. Effortlessly the plane lifted on the ground - we were airborne.

Three scheduled passes were made flying south to north so as have the open door facing the airport building and hangers below. The first was for a simulated re-supply drop. Two large ammunition like boxes - supply bundles - had been maneuvered into place, parachutes attached them, and they attached, like the men would be, a static line [rip cord] to a cable running above the length of the benches to the open door. The radio man talking to the pilot conveyed to the Jump Master when we were over the drop area and the boxes were pushed out the door. The next pass, again at an elevation of about one thousand feet was done so that a wind drift indicator could be sent down. Satisfied with what the wind drift indicators told them, the final pass, once again at low elevation, the men would jump.

Ghost like in appearance, Ralph Spina, veteran World War II paratrooper, sits opposite the World War II paratroopers.
© 2002 Timothy L. Parks

The late Jack Finney, author of many books - Invasion of the Body Snatchers, one you might remember - wrote one entitled *Time and Again* It is science fiction and is all too delightful to read and ponder; and if you do not mind, to read time and again. In it, time travel to the past is achieved by recreating a specific era in time by setting up a stage with authentic buildings, people dressed in the trappings of that time and those same people posing and doing all manner of living as it was done in during period time. The notion being that if authentic enough, the participants willing enough, time travel would occur. You'll have to read the book.

Inside this aircraft as one looked around it became very hard to recognize anything that had to do with December 7, 2002. It was all 1944. The paratroopers with their hats ands chin straps on all began to look like someone's young son gone to war. What little of the ground could be seen through the small streaked windows and the one open door did not look familiar anymore. The sound of the vintage aircraft began to sound as though it was the latest and the best America had. The tight bond among all the men could be felt. There was tension in the air. There was talk and some pep chants made in response to the Jump Master's leading voice, but as the time grew closer for the jump, it grew increasingly quiet and a stillness set in.

On command, a muffled sound emanating from the front of the plane came as the second to the last man who would jump yelled out his number fourteen and saying okay. It was noisy, but the faint spoken numbers and okay could be heard as they began to count down front of plane to back. Each man yelled out and their individual voices become louder and more distinct as the numbers became smaller, the voices closer to the Jump Master who would, who always would be the last man to jump. "... six okay ... five okay ... four okay ... three okay ... two okay" and the first man who would jump out the door yelled very loudly "one okay Jump Master!". The command was given and the last man to grant his willingness to jump was the first man out the door. Anxious to go each man was almost pushed out the door by the man behind him, the Jump Master standing behind and to the left as the line of men grows shorter and shorter until without a sound the Jump Master too had jumped out the door. Michael Zozula by the way was the first one out the door just as he said would likely be.

A strange quiet enveloped the cabin. No one spoke. The drone of the engines lulled on, air from the open door moved about the cabin and the small sounds of flight persisted. I looked over at Richard, at Ralph and at the photographer. The look on their faces, mine too I suspect, was one of a distant satisfaction. Now I would not go repeating this to too many people, in fact I have said nothing to anybody until now, but there for a few moments, I am not so sure we stayed in the skies above Gainesville, December 7, 2002. The pilot may have strayed off course, if you know what I mean. Gradually some talk ensued between the four of us remaining in the cabin. Big and open, hollow from the flight deck to the tail section the seemingly non existent pilot and copilot brought the "Boogie Baby" back to The Gainesville Municipal Airport, the soft landing hardly noticeable.

Roger Wolf, Jump Master, last man out the door, when I had asked him if he had anything to tell me responded in his own words about the jump, about the WWII Airborne Demonstration Team. "Well, like I say, [pause] I'm proud to be here, I'm proud to be here to represent these men that fought the wars. I can't do enough, this is one dedication I do to honor these men which to me is not enough I'm sure, [pause] but when you walk along and they come up to you just crying and see that you're representing them and it brings back memories to them; that's my reward, that's my reward to see these men proud, live again what they done years ago to make us free. [pause] This is for the men that are alive and the men that are gone. This is why we do it right here. This is my mission for these men to show them that I appreciate them." I felt so proud for Roger and all the team. All morning long all I saw were these nineteen men showing kindness, compassion, a genuine interest and respect to each and every person that approached them with stories and questions.

To all of the WWII Airborne Demonstration Team that were here on Saturday ... Christopher J. Stark, Danny Brannock, David Bruce Gordon ,George A. Hicks, Jack B. Dyre, James Cuthbertson, Jan M. Patronek, Jess L. Hicks, Josh Henniger, Magee Brennon, Matthew W. Anderson, Michael A. Zozula, Michael Brent Tomlinson, Michael C. Zozula , Paul Riser, Ray Cunningham, Richard S. Wolf, Robert L. Yarberry, Roger L. Wolf, Terry W. Poyser, Thomas C. Mason ... we extend a sincere thanks and may God Bless you, the Veterans you pay tribute to and may God Bless America.

The C47 "Boogie Baby" was flown back into time by pilot Ray Cunningham.

Preparing to jump.
© 2002 Timothy L. Parks

Ralph Spina left behind as the paratroopers have made their jump
into a sky split by time -- "Boogie Baby" flying in the skies
of the 1940's, spectators on the ground in the year
2002 looking up and into he past.

SANTA FE DEPOT

The Sante Fe Depot as it stood then, not so long after it was built.
Courtesy of StarrBooks

The Sante Fe Depot now, this photograph captured December 2004.

Sante Fe Depot

The year was 1902 when the stone and brick Sante Fe Depot was built in Gainesville. It stands now very much as it did then: A structure with a Mission Revival Architectural theme, the design actually developed by Sante Fe Chief Engineer C.F.W. Felt.

The new constructed depot did not, however, mark the arrival of rail service to Gainesville. It was 14 years earlier on January 2nd of 1887 when the first Gulf, Colorado and Sante Fe passenger train arrived in Gainesville.

A small, wood framed, single story structure was originally built on that parcel of ground sold to the AT&SF by J. M. Lindsey of Gainesville. It served as Gainesville's train depot until the stated intentions of President Manvel came to pass. Manvel, President of Atkinson, Topeka and Sante Fe, said in 1890, "a large and handsome new depot of stone and brick would be built."

It was a desire to compete that brought about the construction of rail lines to Gainesville. It was the need to connect western America that would motivate completing the laying of track connecting together Chicago and the Midwest ... Galveston and the Gulf ... California and the Western United States. All were linked by three railroads working with each other for the common cause. Gainesville was one of the last connections in making those links a reality.

Atkinson Topeka and Sante Fe - AT&SF- is best known today as one of the three railroads involved. Yet even that name, like the other two, now has begun to fade into history. Today, it is the Burlington Northern and Sante Fe -BN&SF- that runs its freight trains through Gainesville.

In the newly built Sante Fe Depot of 1902, along with all the necessary space and services to satisfy the essentials of railroad travel, there was also a Harvey House replete with living quarters for the Harvey Girls and the manager. For almost 30 years, railroaders and passengers enjoyed the fine and unique personalized service offered by Harvey Houses in Sante Fe train depots all over the country.

From its peak in the twenties, through the busy period during World War II, passenger rail service began to fall off in Gainesville, as it did most everywhere. Sante Fe rail service was handed over to Amtrak in 1973. "Lone Star" passenger service to Gainesville and the Sante Fe Depot sadly was ended by Amtrak in 1979.

But that was not the end of the story!

Because of the insight of a few who seized an opportunity, by the hard work of many, and with the donations of Gainesville's generous, the vacated Sante Fe Depot of 1979 still stands today renovated and alive with activity.

AT&SF, after requests and much discussion, donated the Sante Fe Depot to the City of Gainesville in 1981. Ideations as what to do with it and how to best utilize it were passed around for a number of years after its acquisition. Finally, in 1988 renovation began. It would be 2001 before total completion was realized. Sante Fe Depot is now actively operated as a museum, as city offices, and of course as a depot - resumption of Amtrak service came back in 1999. From Oklahoma City to Fort Worth and back, Gainesville is a major stop along the way for the daily "Heartland Flyer".

Late at night lying in bed, train whistles pierce the still air. Low rumbling sounds of the huge diesel locomotives come from afar, get louder, and then pass on to the north or to the south. Somehow the sounds of the trains are tranquil and comforting. How well could one sleep if no trains passed through Gainesville and the nights were still and quiet?

Writers Note:

We are grateful to Mayor Loch and Margaret Hays for working back in the eighties to acquire and preserve our depot. Without their efforts there might be no depot at all. Thank you to Ann Crisp and the Morton Museum for helping provide particulars about the Santa Fe Depot. To learn more about the history of the railroad in Gainesville, visit the museum in the Sante Fe Depot created and run by the Morton Museum.

During operating hours at the Sante Fe Depot Museum, it is Ann Crisp
who will tend to your needs and answer questions.
© 2004 Timothy L. Parks

BOHLS

Young businessman, Clyde Bohls.
Clyde would come to be known in Cooke County first for his management of the of old Kress Store at California Street and Commerce Street ... remember Saturday nights? Then for his time spent as a volunteer fireman, as a successful and innovative business man ultimately building, owning, and operating Bohl's Furniture, and as a man of vision in doing so much for Gainesville during the time he served on the City Council and after. That vision brought manufacturing to Gainesville; Weber was one of those firms. Clyde was instrumental in the forming and creation of the Gainesville Housing Authority.
Courtesy of Dorothy Bohls

Clyde Bohls at his 95th birthday celebration.
© 2004 Timothy L. Parks

Clyde and Dorothy Bohls.
© 2004 Timothy L. Parks

Bohls Furniture store under construction. Constructed in 1959, the structure was built utilizing a method called lift slab, the first structure to be built in this manner in Cooke County. The upper floor and roof structure were cast in place on the bottom floor and then separated as one was lifted off the other and set in place, secured by cast in place collars welded to vertical columns.

Courtesy of Dorothy Bohls

Bohls Furniture Store stands empty, sold in 2006.
The 'lift slab' structure as Clyde said would,
"last forever"

© 2006 Timothy L. Parks

John Ware
Courtesy of Jack Ware

September the 22

Mr ware a gow want
to no the particulars of
your ware Death and
his officers That the low
nolle he Died in fort smith
at the hous of Samel acurry
in the month of January
a Cout the first I Dont
recolect the Date he was
in Coptin _____
John wesly ____
press company he was
not in any redgment
he was inshered Servis
the same was and retta
_____ of _____
_____ that is all
I no a Cout I you will
be lurd what that kind
of Servis means by asking
a united Sats _____

Death Letter
Courtesy of Jack Ware

Death Letter

The year was 1865 when word was received John Ware had died. The letter came to Mrs. Ware some eight months after his death. He was 49 or 50 years old. The death letter (see image) sent to his wife Nancy reads ...
September the 22

Mrs. Ware
You want to no the fertile fears of John Ware death and his officers that he served under. He died in Fort Smith at the hows of Daniel Canedy in the month of January about the first. I don't recollect the day. He was in Captain Tuff, John Wesley Tuff, express company. He was not in any ridgment. He was on secret serves. The arme was under the control of General McNeal. That is all I no about it. You will learn what kind of servis means by asking a United Sats officer.
    A.L. Meddox

The letter was dated in September. John's death was noted as being in the month of January, but no year is to be found. In the family bible, the year 1865 is recorded.

Who was John Ware and what is known of him.

Not a lot.

John was born in Missouri in the year 1915. His father was Isaiah Ware, his mother Elizabeth. John married Nancy Bulger July 1,1841. They had nine children - six of them born in Missouri, the other three in Cooke County, Woodbine, Texas. The oldest was born in 1843. The youngest, who bore his name, was born in 1863. John Ware never did get to see this son.

The Ware family came to the Cross Timbers area of Cooke County in North Texas sometime in the early 1850's. Paperwork to a tract of land - 320 acres - was deeded in 1854 to the Wares. It is a portion of the William Goodnight survey. That property, most of it is still in the Ware family, is located halfway between the Rad A. Ware School in Woodbine and FM 902.

From the death letter several things about John Ware can be determined.

John was very likely a "Red Legged Scout" as was Buffalo Bill Cody in the winter of 1862- 1863, while serving under Captain John Wesley Tuff. These scouts, or as the death letter stated, secret service, performed many hazardous duties hunting undesirables, ferrying dispatches between Forts, that of Dodge, of Gibson, of Leavenworth and others, and carrying out clandestine duties. The "Red Legged Scouts" field of operation was that of northeastern Oklahoma, southwestern Missouri and western Arkansas. They were an independent bunch

As Wild Bill said, "Whenever we were in

Leavenworth, we usually attended all the balls in full force and ran things to suit ourselves."

Was John Ware serving right along side Buffalo Bill? Quite possibly. The time frame is right and the number of men serving in such positions could not have been so great that they would not have at least known each other, and yes, they may well have seen duty together.

In 1863 General McNiel and the men under his command were engaged in driving General Marmaduke's division of Price's Confederate Army out of southern Missouri and across the Arkansas River. Captain Tuff and his secret servicemen served under General McNiel. Wild Bill at this time period had been a scout (a spy in the secret service) under the General, working behind enemy lines disguised as a southern officer from Texas. Is it possible that John Ware too, served as a scout in General McNiel's army?

Of his death, no explanation was given. Maybe it could not be divulged at the time he died? He may not have even died at the house, or if he did, it might well have been of wounds suffered at the hands of the enemy early in the year of 1865.

There is no proof of any of this. There is only the death letter, Buffalo Bill's autobiography, and logic which, when the three are put together, cause it to seem not just plausible, but likely.

Cooke County landowner, husband, father ... how did John Ware end up in the Union Army as a Secret Serviceman?

Prior to his service in the Union Army under Captain John Wesley Tuff, John Ware was living in Cooke County on his property. When war broke out between the

Northand the South it was in his home that polling took place on whether or not to join in secession from the Union. The vote was not in great favor of doing so. It was after this voting that John was faced with the prospect of being arrested and hung by those who opposed he and others considered to be Northern sympathizers.

John fled the Cross Timbers area, headed north and enlisted in the Union Army. It is believed he fled on horseback or by wagon. Many of the men sought after were arrested, he was one of the few that eluded capture and thereby survived what likely would have been his death at the end of a rope at the Great Hanging in Gainesville.

Writers Note:

The descendants of John Ware still live in the Cross Timbers area of North Texas. The Wares of Cooke County number at least six generations now. The deed to the property, the death letter, and the only known picture of John Ware came from the attic of a house on the Ware property. I offer much appreciation to the Wares for contributing much of the information and photographs for this column.

August 2006: John Ware's image used in Death Letter I was later told by one person is that of his son, John Ware, born to John and Nancy Ware, May 7, 1863. No known image of John Ware senior exists this person told me. Faced with conflicting information I have allowed the image to remain. It is either John Ware senior, or a probable likeness of him in his son John Ware.

Buffalo Bill
Courtesy Photograph

CHAINSAW SCULPTURE

Eric Geyer looks through the wings of his not quite completed chain saw
sculpture.
© 2004 Timothy L. Parks

Completed and let loose, the silhouetted eagle appears to have
just landed atop an old tree trunk.

Chainsaw Sculpture - Symbol Freedom

With two chain saws - one small, one large - Eric Geyer brought life to a dead tree. Situated in Leonard Park between Frank Buck Zoo and the pool, the tree rather than being removed, under suggestion by Patrick McCage with the City of Gainesville Parks and Recreation, was turned into a wood sculpture. He called Eric asking if he would turn the hard, dead wood of the old oak tree into something special. Eric does chainsaw sculpting as a hobby, has done so for quite a number of years.

He creates only for special occasions and circumstances that warrant the firing up of those two-cycle chain saw engines - he never does so for hire. It is a passion, the inner desire of an artist that drives Eric. Eric said "yes", and the Saturday before Father's Day he moved into Leonard Park with his familiar Eric's Snack van, his tools, and a determination to create what was decided would be an eagle. Eric moved to Gainesville sixteen years ago from Illinois. "Gainesville", said Eric, "has been good to me, to my family, to our businesses. I love it here and this is my way of saying thanks to the community."

Not alone in his dedication to the project he had a trusted companion, James Lanham who spent the entire weekend with Eric assisting him in every way. James is an employee of Gainesville Parks and Recreation Department. The scaffold Eric stood upon all day Saturday and Sunday, a combined eighteen hours, was donated for use. One set brought in by Jay Cason, a general contractor and the other set provided by David Parson who does home remodeling. Joe Walters Lumber donated the generous number of two by ten scaffold planks needed to top off the elevated work area in a manner making it very safe for Eric so he might concentrate on the art of creation. And the eagle used to model his sculpture after ... well it was donated - not loaned - to Eric by Otts Furniture.

It is a fine thing Eric did spending his Father's Day carving America's symbol of freedom and democracy out of a great, but dead, old oak tree. Fitting it looms so very near Frank Buck Zoo. Gainesville thanks Eric who exemplifies the character of this community - Eric is a Great American!

James Langham, employee of Gainesville Parks and
Recreation Department.
© 2004 Timothy L. Parks

THREE FACES OF THE TURNER HOTEL

Turner Hotel sometime after the turn of the century.
Courtesy the Cooke of County Heritage Society

Turner Hotel as looked in the 1940's.
Courtesy of StarrBooks.

Three Faces of the Turner Hotel

The year was 1884 when the original Turner Hotel was constructed by David H. Turner and opened for business. Moving to Gainesville from Pilot Point in 1880, he for two years ran the Laclede Hotel before deciding to retire. What was originally to be a six bedroom retirement home built at the corner of California and Jefferson Streets soon became for David another hotel - he was back in the business he had so recently retired from, renting out the rooms of his short lived retirement home. Over the years it was added onto a number of times bringing the total number of rooms to 40. Standing two stories tall, with capacious and airy porches off the rooms of each floor, it was a delightful and popular place to stay in Gainesville in the late 1800's and the early 1900's.

In 1920, it was there at the Turner Hotel that the charismatic Joe Baily emerged from his hiatus from politics and announced his candidacy for Governor of the State of Texas. He lost that election to Pat Neff of Waco.

Sadly, the cozy and quaint wood frame structure

was torn down and in its place a six story brick hotel rose from the site in 1927. Dedicating the new Turner Hotel 1928 was the then Senator Joseph Weldon Bailey. Amenities within the hotel were a café, a barber shop, and something rare ... a phone in every room. "Turner Hotel and Restaurant" is how the business advertised itself in Eunice Brown's seventh grade class book of 1955 entitled *Wagon Wheels*.

Billy Turner was the last Turner to run the Hotel and did so for many years. He and his staff were adored by many both for the services the Turner Hotel offered and for their excellent skills and genuine hospitality.

Today, the Turner Hotel is owned and run by the Gainesville Housing Authority, a political subdivision of the City of Gainesville. It was purchased from the Felderhoff's - Tommy, Norbert, and August, - and T. I. Sanders, an oilman from Ardmore, Oklahoma in 1979, completely renovated, then re-opened in 1981 as a retirement home. Self sustaining and successfully run, the Hotel today claims to be Gainesville best value in retirement living.

Writer's Note:
For their assistance, a special thanks to Shana Powell at the Morton Museum, Ann Crisp at the Sante Fe Deport Museum and Jerry Henderson at the Gainesville Housing Authority.

Turner Hotel just as it looked one recent evening.
© 2004 Timothy L. Parks

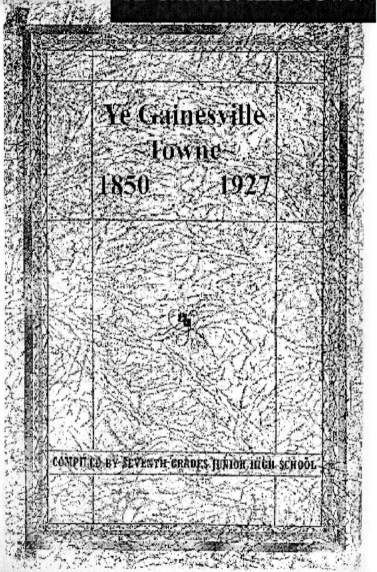

Ye Gainesville Towne
© 2004 Timothy L. Parks

Wagon Wheels

© 2004 Timothy L. Parks

Ye Gainesville Towne

The year was 1927 when the following words became indelible as part of the preface in a book on the history of Gainesville. Those words read:

"In undertaking this work, the authors well realize the difficult task at hand. But the urgent need of a complied history of the community has spurred us on to action. We find hardly a trace of the past history of Gainesville in the public library. Only a few manuscripts and newspaper clippings are available. No published work of this kind has ever been attempted for this city."

The name of that book? *Ye Gainesville Towne*

One might surmise that there was more than one person writing this book as the preface did state authors. Indeed there was. In fact there were about 155 of them. They were the 7th grade students of Gainesville in the year of 1927.

Dorothy (Wingert) Bohls, then a seventh grade student contributed a piece to it called the "Bicycle Club".

It is found on page 50 under Interesting People.

"Mrs. Brien Bonner", says Dorothy, "was our English teacher, Junior High, 1927. She thought up the project of her kids going around interviewing a lot of the elderly people still living. We interviewed them about different subjects and events that had transpired in Gainesville. She sent me out to see about the Bicycle Club."

Indebtedness is given in large part to Mrs. Brien Bonner, English teacher for her "enthusiastic and heavy cooperation". In her Teachers Foreword Mrs. Bonner stated, "The natural expressions of the children have not been curbed and only the most outstanding mistakes have been corrected."

After the book was published, Dorothy said, " we were tickled we wrote in a book." Dorothy is, I assure you, still tickled at this accomplishment!

And what a book it was ... and still is. _Ye Gainesville Towne_ has been referenced by many either in general research or in pursuing some written endeavor. The History of Cooke County, A Pictorial Essay complied by Frank Parker and James Smallwood in 1975 is such an example.

I trust well the unbridled and unbiased veracity of these seventh graders to have reported the history just as they were told. Perhaps the memories of those older folks interviewed were memories that have changed over the years of their long lives, some small instances of embellishment might possibly have occurred - so what. What is history - most of it - but that which is conveyed from the recollection and perspective of people or persons who were there or knew some one who was.

The year was 1955 when once again a book was published by the young people of Gainesville, seeking to record stories of Gainesville's history. This publication was entitled *Wagon Wheels* and was written by the 7th grade students of Miss Eunice Brown's Social Studies Class. Referenced as one of the sources for some of the stories was ... you guessed it, *Ye Gainesville Towne*. Once again, with the exception of a few minor changes, the stories appear just as they were written by the 30 students.

Eunice Brown wrote in her teachers foreword: "The compiling of material and the collecting of funds for the publication of this little booklet has not been an easy task for thirty seventh grade students whose ages average twelve years. They have worked faithfully, and they have a right to be proud of the work they have done."

Ye Gainesville Towne is made up of two parts; the times before 1927 and then their present time period of 1927. It covers a wide range of subjects in both sections - people, buildings, places and events, whereas *Wagon Wheels* is made up of mostly stories pertaining to the history of Cooke County and Gainesville during the period of time prior to 1905.

It is now the year 2004 and the past is loose and getting away. It has been almost fifty years since a class of young people have banded together to record the history of their town. Remember those words ... "We find hardly a trace of the past history of Gainesville ..." There is plenty to write of concerning the past fifty-four years. One could easily go back 70 years, I am certain not much has been recorded from the 1930's to date.

People who were young in 1927 and in 1955 remember much that most of us would not know a thing about. Buildings have been torn down, some have been saved and restored, new ones have been constructed. The face of Gainesville has changed dramatically since 1927. There is a plethora of stories and facts on the people, the places and the events of the last seventy years waiting to be written down and recorded forever for our enjoyment now and for those in the future to reflect upon. But they will not wait forever.

I would challenge the teachers and seventh grade students to do such a thing again.

Next door, across the street, in the nursing home down the way, there is some elderly person living near each of us. You may know him or her. You may not. Introduce yourself. State your cause. Most will want to talk at length and it might be surprising what they remember that has already been forgotten, lost in the whirlwind of the present we live in each day.

First it will be the hunt for the stories. The hunt is always the best part of anything. Then writing the stories and compiling them. Finally, publishing the book and the satisfaction of having written something that has legs and will wander forever would make it all worth while.

Writer's Note:

Special thanks to Mrs. Dorothy Wingert Bohls. Both Ye Gainesville Towne and Wagon Wheels are rare and hard to find books, for they are cherished and held tight by those who have a copy. Recently, both have been published again and are available at your local bookstore, StarrBooks. The students and their teacher mentors did something to record history and in turn they and their books have become a part history. For all of you who contributed to Ye Gainesville Towne and Wagon Wheels, we as a community owe a great deal of indebtedness for this wonderful present day glimpse of the past.

Dorothy Bohls
© 2004 Timothy L. Parks

First Snow

Looking East on California Street, February, 2002

© 2002 Timothy L. Parks

First Snow

Well the weather outside is frightful,
but the fire is so delightful.
Since we got no place to go,
let it snow, let it snow, let it snow.

'The year was 2003, when one afternoon early in February, there came an Arctic front down from the north ushering in cold air ... and snow.

Believing the weatherman that morning, I told my wife to go ahead and make the drive to Denton for her afternoon dental appointment. The storm, I said, was not due into North Texas til later, likely it would be evening when it arrived. I spoke with a measure of confidence as an assurance that I knew as much or more than the weatherman.

Weathermen do prevaricate. Seldom do they own up to it the next day, in fact, they report the past days weather as if they had it pegged in their forecast. Worse than your average duplicitous weatherman, is a Texas weatherman

- one simply cannot predict Texas weather. But they try!
Even worse is the individual - myself for instance - who
believes the authoritative Texas meteorologist, passes on
to another that prognostication, even adding one's own
backwoods intuition to it.

Kathie was sitting in the dental chair that afternoon
of February 4th. The sky had become grey, the air stiffly
cold. Shortly thereafter snow began falling, clinging to
everything, sticking to cold windshields and pavement
alike. Her dentist, not having gotten very far into the work
at hand, called off the appointment and said she was leaving,
going home before the storm hit. You might want to do the
same she told Kathie. They both left. Kathie making her
way north on Interstate 35 home to Gainesville.

Much of the University had deserted the campus.
They too heading out in all directions upon word the storm
was coming.   The school closed due to the impending
winter weather. Just as a few of us, in my department,
had done in the year 2000 when an ice storm settled in
one December afternoon, the same few of us again waited
too long before departing. We had to take an unofficial
assigned position on the crowded highways heading single
file, at a snails pace, in the direction of our homes. A
penalty of sorts for thinking we knew Texas weather better
than even the weathermen we so gleefully bash when they
get it wrong

I was enjoying the sudden whiteness of the road, the
fields, and the sky even as I thought of my wife out there
somewhere. Was she ahead of me in traffic? If behind me,
I hoped it was not too far. Maybe she had not left yet, I did
not know.

Unlike the ice storm of 2000, the snow of 2003 did

not so severely cripple traffic that we were on the road for hours. That ice storm of 2000 was really slick. It took a full two and a half hours for me to make the
30 miles from Denton to Gainesville. This time it was a little more than an hour before I could take that California Street exit and pull into Gainesville.

Leaving the snaking snarl of slow moving traffic on the slick snow packed road I emerged heading east on California Street. It looked so peaceful. It was. The few vehicles that were out moved slow and sure. People afoot were infatuated with the deliberate transformation from wet and grey to frozen and white. As a good snowfall should do, life in Gainesville had slowed down to the very calm pace we all long for.

In the quiet of the dimming light of day the snow was still falling.

I found Kathie waiting for me at the house. She had just arrived having been on the road ahead of me. Anxiety from the tense drive home and worry of one another left us. She climbed Into the 19' motor home I had driven to work this day, and away we went. To eat. To stop by the houses of friends. To drive the silent streets. The only sounds were that of an idling motor and our tires making a hushing noise in the fresh snow. Gainesville is never so deserted or so peaceful except in times such as this white solace.

The next day the University of North Texas was closed due to the weather. That announcement coming late the night before was not unexpected. Snow had ceased to fall, but it was cold and five inches of snowfall remained. Once again we got into the motor home and drove about town. The weight of the vehicle and its dual wheels made for sure footing and stable, safe driving on an otherwise dubious road.

Lunch time approaching, we picked up a few friends and headed east to Woodbine and a small cafe where, as expected, we were the only ones there. We ate well, we talked much, the day was wonderful!

Years ago, I lived in Southwestern Colorado. In the fall, after the leaves had turned golden and fallen to the forest floor, those leafless aspen trees waited. So did the great conifers. The San Juan Mountains waited. I waited. Waited for what? The first snow of the year that would blanket the mountains with snow measured in feet and in the high valleys below with eight, ten perhaps twelves inches or more of the white stuff.

I, like a child on Christmas Eve, did not wait well. I would sleep lightly, get up often, and go out to inspect the sky above. That "first snow" as I recall was the one to cover everything timberline down to high desert and elevations in between.. It usually came mid to late in the fall and in my mind seemed always to come late at night or very early in the morning. I would be there to greet it, watch it fall, and then at the first light of day go out in it.

I cannot fully explain it ... the first snowfall, any blanketing snowfall. There's just something about that peaceful and pure white world.

Writers Note:

Yes, I'm dreaming of a white Christmas. Aren't you? I give thanks to God above for the weather; capricious by design, unpredictable by man, a thing of beauty for all.

Early in the winter of 1979 along the Dolores River in the
San Juan Mountains of Southwestern Colorado.

First Presbyterian Church Live Nativity 2004

Christmas in Gainesville

The year was 1969 when so many of us, young and old alike, sat in front of the television and watched an animated version of one of America's most beloved comic strips. The show was *A Charlie Brown Christmas*. In it, we found who else but Charlie Brown, befuddled and depressed, trying to cope with the commercialization and lack of meaning Christmas had somehow taken on.

Vicariously, through one or more of the characters, we each shared the disgust, the sad emptiness, and an inability to grasp the true meaning of Christmas in the midst of so much hyperbole regarding Santa Clause, bright lights, and extravagant gifts. We too searched.

None the less, it was then still the meaning of Christmas we searched for. Now, Christmas is being replaced with the word "holiday" or some other meaningless, generic term so as not to offend those who object to celebrating Christmas for what it is and for what it always has been. Christmas, the day and the period of time around it, is being redefined to celebrate a mixed bag of beliefs and traditions, ideas and ideals, most of which have nothing to do with Christ. Unfortunately, as each year goes by, there is becoming a disregard for Christmas altogether. We should not be depressed as Charlie Brown was, rather we should be angered. As we witness more and more subtle and furtive abductions of Christmas and its true meaning, the stronger our understanding of it, our faith in it, and our resolve to hold it close and safe becomes.

Here in Gainesville, as they have done for the last twenty some years, the First Presbyterian Church put on a Live Nativity scene. Different from all years past, this year, rather than just going out and taking their places around the manger and barn, the actors converged upon the barn made of hay bales from disparate places just as it had occurred more than two thousand years ago.

From the northwest, Joseph and Mary plodded along coming to an Inn at Bethlehem and finding no room they settled for the night into a barn with the new born Jesus. From the northeast, following a bright star, three Wise Men found their way to the barn where away in a manger Jesus had lay down his sweet head. From the south, shepherds who had been watching their flocks in the fields came upon the small gathering and joined the semi circle of all those who had come to marvel at the sight of the baby Jesus.

Angie Hare, Reverend John Hare's wife said , "it made me cry when I looked to the north and saw the approaching procession of Joseph and Mary, two donkeys, a couple of goats and sheepherders."

It had grown dark when all had arrived at the barn and manger. There were it seemed a multitude of heavenly hosts and among many people who had traveled to the site from all over Cooke County.

Angie's sister Pam as she took it all in exclaimed, "I just love a small town".

We are fortunate to live in Gainesville where events like this are still possible and welcomed by the community. Just a little more than a week before the Live Nativity, what is now an annual event took place: Journey to Bethlehem.   Thursday evening, December 2nd, the sidewalks along California Street and those surrounding the Courthouse were crowded. People made their way in and out of shops while pausing at each biblical scene put on by an area church of which there were eight this year. Margaret Bewley, Vice President of the Downtown Development Association (downtown store merchants) and owner of Chapman's, had done some research and created this Christmas celebration for Gainesville.   A brilliant idea with instant appeal, it is only two years old and in the minds of many already a tradition.

Near the end of *A Charlie Brown Christmas*, Linus stepped out onto the stage and began to speak. Out of the mouth of an animated boy - a thumb sucking, blanket carrying, precocious youngster - from memory he recited scripture from Luke.

> *And there were in the same country shepherds, abiding in the field, keeping watch over their flock by night. And, lo, the angel of the Lord came upon them, and the glory of the Lord shone round about them! And they were sore afraid. And the angel said unto them, "Fear not! For, behold, I bring you tidings of great joy, which shall be to all my people. For unto you is born this day in the city of David a*

Savior, which is Christ, the Lord. And this shall be a sign unto you: Ye shall find the babe wrapped in swaddling clothes, lying in a manger."

And suddenly, there was with the angel a multitude of the Heavenly Host praising God, and saying, "Glory to God in the Highest, and on Earth peace, and good will toward men." (Luke 1:8-14)

It got real quiet both on the television and in living rooms all over America ...

Then Linus said, "That's what Christmas is all about, Charlie Brown."

The entire Peanuts Gang then sang *Hark the Herald Angels Sing.*

To the crowd gathered at the Live Nativity the Reverend John Hare spoke. In praise of the Lord and on behalf of First Presbyterian Church he offered the Live Nativity as a gift to all. At the Reverend's suggestion we all sang *Away in a Manger.*

It was beautiful!

That's what Christmas is all about, my friends.

Merry Christmas Gainesville and Cooke County!

Writers Note:

We are lucky to live in Gainesville, a community full of churches of faith and strength. Abundant thanks to the First Presbyterian Church; it's Reverend, its members and especially those who stood silently and stoically portraying for us the birth of our Lord and Savior Jesus Christ.

Charlie Brown and Snoopy
Courtesy Photo

The Cates Men - Luther, Luke and Willis (left to right)
Courtesy of Luther Cates

Two Brothers in the 86th Blackhawk Infantry Division at Camp Howze

The year was 1943 when Luther Cates's brother Willis was about to be drafted into the Army. It was the first draft of young men 19 and 20 years old and he would be in that draft. Luther had plans to go to Pearl Harbor and do Naval construction work. Clearance from the government had been granted, he had a ticket to Vallejo, California - all he had to do was get a release from the draft board.

"The draft board refused to release me," said Luther. "I found out Willis was about to be drafted, so I went down and volunteered for the service to go with him, so we could go together."

Luther was born in June of 1924. Willis, 15 months older than he, was born in March of 1923. Their parents lived in Amarillo, Texas at the time he was born. A strict Kentuckian, his mother said she wasn't going to have a child born in Texas, so she rode the train from Amarillo back to Kentucky. Luther was born in Providence,

Kentucky, a little coal mining town. Unlike Luther, Willis did not have to make a long, bouncing trip by train to Kentucky - he was born there before the family moved to Amarillo.

"My dad, Luke, was a coal miner", Luther states, "I still can't sing, but I'm a coal miner's son." Luther laughs.

Luke left Kentucky because he had asthma so bad. Arizona was to be the families destination, but they never made it that far west. Stopping in Amarillo to visit an Uncle, his asthma started clearing up so they stayed on longer, and then a little longer, and the next thing he had gone to work for his Uncle. They never left.

"He was in the retail end of the furniture business from the day I was born until the day he died," Luther said of his father.

Before arriving at Camp Howze, Willis and Luther first went to Camp Walters at Mineral Wells. One morning they began calling out the names of men who would be shipped out, going north to Camp Howze for further training. Willis's name was called, Luther's was not hollered out.

"I went over to ask them if my name was called. They said presently they had me scheduled to go to the Air Corps in Florida. I said, I don't want to go in the Air Corps, I want to go to the same place he's going. They called me back a few hours later and said I would follow him in about 2 days. We both ended up at Camp Howze, Texas northwest of Gainesville. He was in the infantry, I was in the artillery - we were both in the same 86th Blackhawk Infantry Division."

Leaving Camp Howze late in the year - sometime in

November - Willis went on maneuvers in Louisiana. He had moved on without and after Luther. From Louisiana, his division was split up to fill other divisions - he stayed on to help train the new soldiers coming in. He then was transferred to Camp Chaffee in Arkansas for additional training, until the time he was scheduled to go to the South Pacific. Abruptly, the decision was made to send more troops into Europe because the war was going well and they needed to keep pushing the Germans. His division was part of the now famous Battle of Cologne, they were utilized to close up the rear pocket. His division joined the 15th Army, then were combined with the 1st Army before finally joining Patton's 3rd Army. They made the drive south with the 3rd and that's where Willis's Division was when the war ended.

Shortly before Willis had left for Louisiana, Luther had transferred into the Air Corps - he ended up flying after all, as a member of the 394th Bomb Group of the 584th Squadron in the 9th Air Force. He was the radioman, as well as waist gunner on a B-26 Marauder. His group flew their missions out of Cambrai in the Northern part of France.

B26 Martin Marauder
Dorothy Bohls

"You see," said Luther, "They had the top turret,

and they had the tail turret - the tail gunner and the top gunner. Then there were two guns, one on each side of the plane at the waist. All of the guns, 11 altogether, fixed or manned, were 12.7 mm machine guns. A waist gunner did not man a particular side, he could shoot out from either side of the plane."

The B-26 Marauder was a high speed medium bomber with a normal bomb load of 3000 pounds, however capable of being loaded up with an additional 1000 pounds on the wings. It had a range of 1,100 miles and its maximum speed was 283 mph. Twenty versions of the plane were made and 5,157 of the aircraft were built by the Martin Company. It was used primarily in close tactical ground support, but served in a variety of mission types including photo reconnaissance. Among its nicknames was Widow-Maker, the least deserved and actually an oxymoron in that the B-26 went on after early refinements to serve in the Air Corp's 9th Air Force with the lowest attrition rate of any American aircraft. It was not unlike the A-7 Warthog we know of, serving so well in the Gulf War.

"We were never shot down. We were thankful", said Luther, "There had been a lot of shots taken at us, but we only got hit one time. There wasn't much damage, just rocked our plane, scared us."

Luther tells of a close call while in the air ....

"Towards the end of the war, whenever we had the Germans pocketed in, we would fly over and drop circulars with information explaining what would happen if they surrendered; in fact tell them to surrender, and what the terms would be.

We were on one of those missions, what we call

a paper mission. There were three planes that flew out that day.   We were flying in the middle of the formation, one plane went north, one plane went south, we flew dead ahead to drop our 100 pound bombs, loaded with circulars, over our target. I recall that four of the bombs had hung up in the bomb bay - wouldn't go out, somebody had wired them in wrong. I had to get down in the bomb bay to clear them. I got in, but had my parachute on just in case I fell out, for the bomb bay doors were open. I started kicking these bombs, they were dropping down and coming up, dropping down and coming up, and I'd kick em' when they would come up. I didn't think about the little propeller in front of each bomb going around and around and around - that was the fuse. Well, one of them blew off and when it did a good portion of the paper hit me in the face, knocking me back across into the rear bomb bay, a bomb bay we seldom used.

Everybody wanted to know what had happened. It scared them to death when they heard that thing go off. The poor tail gunner was covered with paper, it had blown back towards the rear of the plane.   Luckily, I didn't get hit with anything but paper."

The crew asked me, "How did it feel?"

"It was like getting hit with a telephone book right in the face", I told them. They wanted to know if I was hurt. I said, "I think my face is gone", but then I had my eyes closed the whole time. Finally, I reached up and felt my face, I looked at my hand, there wasn't anything wrong. I was just totally numb, that was all!

I looked at the bomb bay, it was clear. So I said, "It's clear, let's leave, let's go home. I was, I believe, the only man in the war that had got blown up in the face by a bomb and didn't even get a purple heart."

World War II ended May 8,1945 and Luther came home from the war on the 19th of that August, he was not to be a career military man. Of course, many did not stay on, they were no longer needed to fight. Their wives and girlfriends needed them back; their home towns needed them back; America needed its men back home working and raising families.

"I was out by December 31st 1945," said Luther, "New Year's Eve, I was gone."

Willis did not make it home from the war. He was killed just north of Munich, about 15 or 20 kilometers to the northeast. Just 5 days before the war ended.

Willis's division had gone into Bavaria and then were pulled right back out. Luther was down there on the 13th of May looking for him. He had no idea at that time Willis was missing in action or had been killed. The war was over and Command was pulling them out and sending them back home to the United States. He happened to see them - Willis' Division - as they came onto the autobahn, but he went on to Munich, then had to turn and come back. Having flown into Stuttgart, Germany from Binlow, Holland, Luther had to get back to his plane and fly back to Binlow.

"I found out ... oh ... I guess several days later that Willis was missing in action, and then I received a telegram from my father stating he had been killed in action."

For awhile Willis was buried there in Nuremberg. His wife brought him back a couple years later and had him buried at Wichita Falls. They had married only five days before he shipped out.

Like his father, Luther went into the furniture business. For 19 years he was a representative and a manufacturing company representative in the retail end of furniture. In August 1971, he started work at The University Texas. He was Building Services Supervisor for Custodial Services for several years and then became the Furnishing and Equipment Coordinator.

"We were self- sufficient", said Luther. "We had our own furniture shop, our own stripper and everything. We could take a piece of furniture and make it look new. When an old building was renovated or torn down, we took the furniture, ran it through our shop, and had it all redone and rebuilt - it came out looking like new. We just reused it all. Anything that was ordered would be additional bookcases, metal file cabinets - that was before computers - and a few new desks."

Calls had been made to many of the large colleges around the country asking exactly how they furnished their faculty with furnishings, equipment and desks. Luther, in his University of Texas shop, was the only one in the entire United States that was self- sufficient.

Luther retired after 17 years and since 1989 lives in Georgetown, Texas.

Asked to share some personal insight about World War II, Luther paused for a moment, reflected, and thoughtfully said, "It was supposed to be the war to end all wars, but we've had a few since then. Maybe we didn't clean up what we thought we should have. Actually we did one thing, we got rid of a tyrant and liberated a bunch of countries, and were very well thought of when the war was over. But anyway, it's just something that we got into. I've been accused of participating in a war without having been attacked or without anybody dropping bombs on us. I said no, but the Germans did declare war on us ... and I said don't forget Pearl Harbor."

Writers Note:

Luther was recently in Gainesville seeking reference material to send to other members of his artillery unit of the 86th Blackhawk Infantry. They're having a reunion in September and he was revisiting the Camp Howze area. Thank you Luther for our time together, for your service to our country, and for the gentle kindness you give so freely.

August 2006: Luther Cates, in the originally published column, was said to have worked at the University of North Texas. He did not, and a correction was made to read the University of Texas.

Luther Cates
© 2004 Timothy L. Parks

Camp Howze Obstacle Course
Courtesy of StarrBooks

REMEMBER THEM

The United States Marine Corps Color Guard with the
Commemorative Air Force above approaching on their
fly over from the south.

Attending Gainesville's Veterans Day Celebration 2004 was
Michael James Moore of Valley View, Texas. He served in
the United States Navy from 1975 until 2000.

© 2004 Timothy L. Parks

Remember Them

The year was 1954 when Congress was urged by various veteran's service organizations to broaden the meaning of Armistice Day. What had been celebrated since 1926 as a holiday to remember the men and women who had fought in World War I, now would be known as Veterans Day. June 11, 1954 President Dwight D. Eisenhower, by the stroke of his pen, signed into law November 11th would from that year forward be celebrated as Veterans Day, a day to remember our veterans from all wars.

It was not so many days ago Veteran's Day, November 11, 2004 was celebrated here in Cooke County at Leonard Park. As five-thirty approached I began to peregrinate west on California Street from StarrBooks on South Commerce Street towards the Cooke County Veterans War Memorial. There were others also trekking that way afoot, many drove. My feet were light, my pace brisk. A North Texas November sky was slowly giving way to dusk, the clouds seemingly darkening, the air becoming still and cold.   Camera in hand, thoughts of great men of our great country were on my mind. I made my way to the Veterans Day Celebration.

Earlier in the day, before leaving my place of work at The University of North Texas I had passed Julius, my immediate supervisor, a Viet Nam War Veteran, in the hall.

"What are you going to do this evening for Veteran's Day?" I asked.

Stern faced he replied, "make the drive home, eat, relax, go to bed. What about you?"

"We're going to the Veteran's Day Celebration," I told him.
"Every year they have a ceremony with patriotic music, a fly over, free barbeque and fireworks."

"They don't do that for the Veteran's in Dallas."

"That's a shame," I said, " makes me proud to be from Gainesville, a small town."

Julius agreed.

I left.

Small town or not it's a grand thing to do for our Veterans. Gainesville, a Medal of Honor City, does it right. The Gainesville V.F.W. Post #1922 does it right. They did so last year and the year before and ... but for a county of thousands I was somewhat disappointed at the few hundred residents turning out to honor our veterans instead of a few thousand. We, the residents of this county and this nation can do better to appreciate them.

We can take the time not just to celebrate those days set aside to honor our men and women in uniform, our veterans, our country, our independence - but to reflect more often on the price paid by so many for the freedom we each enjoy in this country of ours.

I was moved by it all: The United States Marine Corps Color Guard, the Commemorative Air Force Fly Over, the music, and the ceremony. One could not help but feel the severe reverence paid to our veterans and to our flag by all attending. It was exciting to be there.

It brings to mind a piece I would like to share ...

Remember Me?

Some people call me Old Glory, others call me the Star Spangled Banner, but whatever they call me, I am your Flag, the Flag of the United Sates of America ... Something has been bothering me, so I thought I might talk it over with you ...

I remember some time ago people lined up on both sides of the street to watch the parade and naturally, I was leading every parade, proudly waving in the breeze. When your daddy saw me coming, he immediately removed his hat and placed it over his heart ... remember? And you, I remember you standing straight as a soldier. You didn't have a hat but you were giving the right salute. Remember your little sister? Not to be outdone, she was saluting the same as you, with her right hand over her heart ... remember?

What happened? I'm still the same old flag. Oh, I have a few more stars since you were a boy. A lot more blood has been shed since those parades of long ago.

But now I don't feel as proud as I used to. When I come down your street, you just stand there with your hands in your pockets and I may get a small glance, then you look away. I see the children running around and shouting ... they don't seem to know who I am ... I saw one man take off his hat and then look around. He didn't see anybody else with their's off so he quickly put his back on.

Is it a sin to be patriotic any more? Have you forgotten what I stand for and where I've been - Anzio, Korea, Guadalcanal, and Viet Nam. Take a look at the Memorial Honor Rolls sometime, of those who never came back, to keep this republic free ... One Nation Under God ...When you salute me you are actually saluting them.

Well, it won't be long until I'll be coming down your street again. So, when you see me, stand straight, place your right hand over your heart ... and I'll salute you, by waving back ...and I'll know that ... YOU REMEMBERED!!

Writers Note:

To all Cooke County Veterans, to Veterans everywhere I thank and dedicate this column to you. I thank Bill Riley for passing on the piece Remember Me?

Veterans Day 2004 Poster
Courtesy of the Veterans Administration

Astronaut David R. Scott gives a salute to the U.S. Flag
during a 1971 Apollo 15 moonwalk.
Courtesy of the Veterans Administration

Childhood Recollections

Lucy Bradley Junkin
Courtesy of Betty Junkin Guest

Childhood Recollections

'Good aftanoon Mrs. Higgins.   Hot nough for ya'
It's a summer afternoon somewhere in Kansas, Oklahoma, North Texas.
Over on Stone County Road there's the smell of chicken cooking.
The wind is blowing the leaves down the gutter as the mailman comes by.
'Henry! It's gettin' t'awards suppertime ya know. Henry!' ---

> *From the Bloodlines album,*
> <u>*The Pirates of Stone County Road*</u> *by John Stewart*

The year was 2004 when I received in the bookstore mail, a packet postmarked: Lake Dallas, TX 75065 Oct 13, '04. Unassuming, the yellowish orange, clasp envelope sparked little interest as a lot postage and paper is spent in an effort or sell or otherwise convince the small business owner to agree and part with money they do not have. It sat unopened most all that day in October it was delivered.

Inside the envelope, however, was anything but an offer to sell us something. Instead, it turned out to be a real treasure. Betty Junkin Guest had sent along to me two of her mothers writings, one of which appeared in my column back on November 12, 2004 entitled *The Woman of Tomorrow*.

In response to this generous offering I responded to Betty in an E Mail saying, "What a pleasant thing to receive in the mail. An apparition, a treasure from the past came walking right through our door". At the same time I also wrote asking permission to print the two writings by her mother Lucy.

I do believe this is what she had intended, both of us preferring though the exchange of formalities by slow mail and of E Mail before arriving at the foregone conclusion. Betty in kind said yes.

Of that the first writing, the essay *The Woman of Tomorrow* Betty wrote, "Mama was a voracious reader and a surreptitious writer. She loved companionship through reading and story telling, but did not share her writings. I did not know she had given a high school, graduation address - she was third in her class - and discovered it only after he death, written on a Big Chief tablet."

It is of her mothers childhood recollections - what Lucy wrote - that I want to share with you the reader, but Betty, in the letter she sent along with her mother's writings wrote of and touched upon a few of her own childhood memories in Gainesville.

"Gainesville has always had a special place in my

heart", began Betty, "Not only because my maternal roots are there, but also because I spent some of my happiest childhood summer days with my grandparents - Given W. and Eddie Mae Johnson Bradley - in their home at 1411 East California Street during the 1930's and 1940's. The house in no longer there. Without air conditioning, our custom was to sit on the front porch after supper - and it was "supper", our main meal, dinner was at noon - we would sit out on the front porch visiting with neighbors and passers-by. Often my grandmother - Granny- would say, 'Mr. Bradley, let's take a drive down south.'

When I asked Granny why she didn't call my grandfather - whom I called Dada - by his first name like most other wives did, she said, 'I called him Mr. Bradley when we courting and I just don't like changes.' They were married in 1893, having courted since 1890.

So we would drive down Lindsay, Denton and Church Streets. Most often I would ask to finish our drive by going to Watts for ice cream. Granny and Dada seldom denied my requests; so my memories of summer evening treats of Watts ice cream are many. In later years when I was old enough to go to Saturday afternoon matinees at the State Theater, my friends and I would go, after the movie, to Watts for afternoon sodas. I believe the bar stools on which we sat are still there.

How special it is that now I can enjoy my memories of Watts and my love of books all in the same space!"

It strikes me that when we sit with a friend, or a member of our family, how much there is that we might not know about that person we've known for years or perhaps all our lives.

Betty for instance. I had first met her when she was

still in town, active at the First Presbyterian Church. I suppose, like the yellowish gold envelope, I did not regard Betty in the manner I should have. This is how a lot of us go about our lives in dealing with our most cherished of all things - the people in our lives. We do not even realize the hidden treasures sitting there so close by, much less per chance to dig for them. If we listened more and worked at that almost unattainable virtue of patience, in time, the unassuming envelope would likely one day arrive.

Of her mother's *Recollection of Childhood In Gainesville, Texas* Betty wrote, "Not long before she died at 87 years of age, Mama did write down at my urging her recollections of a day and a half in her childhood. She was my mother and I am prejudiced, but I think this remembrance is a masterpiece."

Lucy Bradley Junkin's, Recollection of Childhood In Gainesville, Texas Circa 1906.

The United States, after more than two and a half hundred years of colonizing, winning its independence from European nations, spreading west until it did indeed stretch from shore to shore and fighting a senseless civil war, finally reached maturity in the late 1800's . . . then celebrated coming of age with the Gay Nineties.

At the turn of the century, when I was born, it took its place very comfortably among the world's leading countries. A very fine time to be born, I think. And Gainesville, Texas, a town of less than ten thousand, was an ideal place to be born. For it was there I experienced many associations and situations on which the foundation for my long life was built.

It was from my mother Mrs. Given W. Bradley, nee Eddie Mae Johnson] that I received an interest of all about me -- the first wildflowers in the grass in the spring, the rainbow, the birds -- everything -- including people. She found something of interest in every person she met -- male or female, old or young, black or white. And the way of life in those days in a small town afforded every opportunity to know people. For one thing we were in daily contact with many tradespeople. There were, of course, no super markets; thus we went to various places for our food supplies.

There were several meat markets where we found meat only. Whole carcasses of dressed cows, calves, hogs, and pigs hung in the ice locker. But at busy times, the butcher would leave out hind quarters and fore quarters on his chopping block so that he could cut a roast or steak and such according to his customer's specifications. The fact that I had seen the cow plodding behind the butcher's wagon on the way to the slaughter house the day before did not disconcert me. I had also waited patiently for the wagon with the carcass, covered with a heavy white canvas sheet, to pass on its return to the market. I loved animals, but easily distinguished between those to be loved and those to be eaten.

The butcher always greeted us by name, "Good morning, Mrs. Bradley; hello, Lucy." I was in the first grade with his son and said to Mr. Hogan one time, "Hugh sure can draw good." His father replied, "Yes, we are afraid he'll draw himself out of school." True,

Hugh was not a good student and was usually drawing when he should have been learning how to spell. I wonder where Hugh is now. Is he an artist or does he work in a super store meat department? -- I'm forgetting -- Hugh, if he still lives, is 82.

Other customers came into the market and we said "Goodbye" to Mr. Hogan, exchanged "Good Morning" with the new customers and crossed the street to Merzbacher Bros.

Mr. Leo and Mr. Ed Merzbacher thought of their patrons as their friends. Their shelves were filled with the best foods available and were priced accordingly. The women who appreciated the more choice food traded there. Of course, there were other grocery stores. I can remember some five or six others, all in the business district. There were later a few neighborhood grocery stores. "Merzsbacher's," as it was called, was one of Tyler and Simpson Wholesale Company's best patrons, and my father thought it proper that we patronize them. Papa was with that company as Secretary from its formation about 1890 until he had a massive heart attack and died at once when he was 71 years old. That was Thanksgiving night, 1938. Young Eben [Junkin, Jr., Mama's only son] was then 12 ½ years old, and Betty [Bradley Junkin Guest, Mama's only daughter] was three years younger -- I digress, as is my wont.

Merzbacher's fascinated me, partly because of their candy counter with curved glass top and low shelves of glassed cookie boxes. Both candy and cookies were placed so that a small child could easily see them. I'm sure that they were not accidentally thus placed.

I don't believe it's my imagination when I say that candy equaled in quality anything boxed by Whitman or Stoffers today. It was not cheap. I will not go into the varieties of chocolates except to mention a delicious one with a cream center which Mary [Harris, Mrs. Dewitt Ray] and I called false teeth because of the shape!

Since we were going home, Mama told them to put her purchases in the phaeton where she had already placed the packages of meat. We stopped to chat with friends and "Mr. Ed" held the door open for us. Mama untied the horse from the iron ring in the sidewalk, got in the buggy and "headed for home."

Next morning Mama was going to be busy in the house; so she phoned Merzbacher's and the Meat Market to have deliveries made. We never bought in quantities except staples such as sugar and flour. Our first caller was the milk man -- indeed he came before we were up and about. The night before, Mama had placed the glass quart bottles on the back steps and had tucked a note in one of the bottles to tell him which of his products she needed.

Mama looked to see how much ice we would need for our large ice-box which was on the back porch. It was equipped with a drain pipe so that we didn't have to place a pan under the box for the dripping water as the ice melted. Instead, the pan was placed outside of the house under the end of the pipe. On hot days, red birds, mocking birds and the noisy despised sparrows enjoyed cool sips of water as well as baths. When Mama decided how many pounds of ice she would need, she placed the card marked with large numbers in the window where Mr. Campbell could see it from his wagon. The card was turned to indicate 25 lbs., 50 lbs., 75 lbs., or 100 lbs.

Soon we would hear Mr. Proffer's bell as he drove his "spring" (small, light) wagon loaded with freshly gathered vegetables and fruits to our gate. The land east of Gainesville was known as the "Cross Timbers" and had wonderful sandy soil which was great for the products Mr. Proffer marketed. When I was in High School, later, his daughter was in my class. Country schools did not go beyond the seventh grade.

Rufus Smith, Negro, came that afternoon to mow our lawn. I followed in his footsteps, asking questions every minute which he answered in detail. He told Mama he had to talk to me to keep me from talking myself to death. Rufus worked for us for at least sixty years. He housecleaned, cooked, did simple electrical and plumbing jobs and kept Mama's flower beds. He did the planting, but Mama stood by him telling where and how deep to plant them. She had beautiful roses and the most spectacular sweet peas ever grown in Gainesville. She bought her seeds and plants with great care and spared no expense. Rufus was a wonderful man and was respected by both black and white people . He had a daughter my age by his first wife and later had twelve other children [mostly boys], the youngest being about Eben Jr's age.

That evening Papa moved the porch chairs out to the lawn where it was cooler. Our neighbors did likewise, and there was visiting back and forth. Although we lived on the main street, there was no traffic except on Saturdays when the folks in the country would come in to shop. Some would pass the house going home that night. But there was no danger of being hit by a horse and buggy -- or wagon -- so we were allowed to play in the street, still unpaved. We especially liked to play under the light swung over the intersection. There the "hop toads" gathered and it was great fun to chase them. Of course, we chased fire flies, too.

About ten o'clock we were called in, made to wash our feet! And so to bed. The end of a normal happy day of my childhood.

Writers Note:

My sincere thanks to Betty who helped me to know where treasures are to be found. I agree with Betty - this remembrance is a masterpiece.

Lucy Bradley Junkin
Courtesy of Betty Junkin Guest

South Denton Street then.
Courtesy of StarrBooks

South Denton Street now.
© 2006 Timothy L. Parks

Three soda jerks pause behind the counter while a customer sits probably sipping on a soda. In the early fifties the fountain was still located on the south side of the pharmacy, though its days there were numbered before being moved to the north side. Watts Brothers Pharmacy began operation in 1915.

Courtesy of Connie (Cypert) Stovall

One store owner and two soda jerks pause for the camera as do
three happy customers at the counter.   Bill and Connie Cypert took
over Watts in the early sixties   In July of 2004 StarrBooks moved
their bookstore into the historic Watts Brothers Pharmacy keeping the
fountain, operating and selling unique gifts, all in addition to being
a full service bookstore. The only prescriptions filled, however,
are book prescriptions. Left to right behind the counter are
StarrBooks owner Kathie Parks and soda jerks Vanessa Cabrera
and Angelina English.   On the counter stools left to right are Louis
Stephenson, Georgia Knabe, and Janie Reitz. Janie remembers
summers with her grandparents Blake and Naomi Scott of
Forestburg, Texas. Trips into Gainesville and a stop at
Watts were the highlight of her childhood summers.

Rain & Sand

The year was 1975. The war in Viet Nam is over.

We all have a war. One we fought in, one in which friends or a loved one fought in, worse yet was killed in action, a war remembered vividly and so well for whatever reasons. But we all have a war. Mine was the Viet Nam War.

As it was in Tucson and Pima County where I grew up, it was also in Gainesville and Cooke County: Young men, boys barely out of high school, were inducted into the military and sent off to fight a war that to this day is still not fully understood. I know somewhere in Gainesville or in Cooke County - he may no longer live in these parts - there was another young man my age, just like me whose number was up, but was spared the ordeal.

I was nineteen, my unlucky lottery number very low, and the end of the war stirred many emotions inside of me, not the least of which was the relief I felt in knowing I would not be going away to fight . If called, with that low number, it was not a matter of if, but when I would go. I would have gone as did so many, some of them my friends. Later in life I would learn bits and pieces of the war, first hand experiences from those who served and made it back.

I cannot relate any personal war experiences, I grew up with the war. In Tucson, Davis Montham Air Force Base, had always been used for training pilots. B47's, U2's more recently A4's, the Warthogs as they are known. During the Viet Nam era the pilots flew and trained in the Phantoms, the F4C's as we commonly called them, although there were different versions of the fighter. Pilots trained day and night in the skies over and around the city. The sounds and the sight of the planes engrained in the minds of Tucsonians.

Newspaper headlines and articles reported the war; the battles, the fighting, the wounded, the prisoners taken, the dead. I remember a weekly magazine that had pictures of those who had died in combat the week prior; fighter and bomber pilots, helicopter pilots, so many Army and Marine ground troops. As a young boy, I would lay on the bed with my father reading and looking, just looking, maybe asking redundant questions that he did not have answers to. The war went on for years. Our lives went on. We thought little during the day of those men who were fighting so far away, only to be reminded of it on the evening news.

That was then.

Now... the talk of the Viet Nam war has diminished, we have been in numerous conflicts and wars since, but I still think about that war, read about it maybe more now than in the sixties and seventies. The books I read are written by authors who have taken the time to coax the veterans and then listen to those who are willing to tell of their experiences. Many are not. These are the true eyes and ears of war, the men and woman of valor who faced death each day, who lived under the worst conditions, fought for our country no matter what the odds, without question. These are not books written on certain heroic individuals and they do not deal with the technical aspects of war ... weapon systems; guns, planes, armored vehicles used, nor do they go into great detail on a particular battle; the plans, the objectives, the implementation of the same, and then the results.

Read the book *Nam* (1981) by Mark Baker. It is a book written with the words of the men and woman who fought. No names, just pieces of the war presented in very powerful and profound words. Short thoughts and observations. Long episodes. One short story ended with these words, the words of a young Marine, a boy transformed very quickly into a man. With calm veracity he stated ...

> *"It's hard to believe, but I didn't have a care in the world while I was in Nam. I'd get up in the morning all covered with mud, look up in the sky with the rain splashing in my face and just smile. "I'm alive." The only worry you had was dying, and if it happened you wouldn't know it anyway. So what the heck."*

For some of us, the eventual necessary character building brought on by the juxtaposition of life's unfairness comes slowly over the years in an almost planned out manner. If we are fortunate they come. We have known hunger so that we can walk away from every good meal appreciating it, and be thankful for it.   To be without money makes a job of any kind the best job you've ever had. In our friendships and in marriage we sometimes lose our closest friends, we lose a spouse for whatever reason we are set apart from them. The ones we love again, when we come to love again, that love cherished and held like a treasure. In our loneliest and darkest hour we come to find the Lord again, or for the first time, and begin to understand the imperfection of this world and where all things truly come from. Through it all we make it, we can change our lives because the one thing we as Americans have is the freedom to do so, to cause change of all kinds in our lives.

The soldiers, the men and woman who are on the line, in a very short amount of time come to know the broad spectrum of what life has to offer: hunger, loneliness, the loss of friends and comrades. And at times, like the Marine in Viet Nam, for many it all gets boiled down to appreciating life itself even when death sits close and patiently nearby.

In Iraq it is sand, not rain, that greets the face of the fighting soldier each new day. The sun beats down through a dry air mass and the terrain is a brown desert, not the green, lush jungle setting of Nam.   Discerning who is friend and who are foe seems once again to pose a challenge, however few they may be.   A quandary for soldiers trained to follow rules while possessing compassion.

The men and woman who have gone off to fight the war on terror do so voluntarily; there has been no draft since the Viet Nam War. The two wars are disparate, times have changed, and the reasons our troops have gone off to fight in Afghanistan and Iraq are lucid, the enemy is not, he is elusive and cunning.

The year is 2004 and we have been at war with the terrorists of our world since 2001. They, this silent, clandestine enemy would not think twice at killing any one of us or our family members either in masse or one at a time, by any means they can carry out their sadistic and mad plan. The year when the War on Terror will end is not in sight.

> *Writer's Note:*
> *I personally thank all of the men and woman who have fought our wars, who are now fighting this war. Our thoughts, our prayers are with them. They have stood, and they stand today, between us and an unfairness of life we as a free people need not come to know - the loss of our freedom and democracy.*

Old Glory flaps in the breeze above the flag of this Great State of Texas.

© 2004 Timothy L. Parks

My Name is Old Glory

The year was 1923 when Cooke County, along with the rest of the country, adopted June 14th as Flag Day. And on that day, like the Army and Navy, the whole nation adopted the U.S. Flag Code so as to use the proper procedure in handling the flag.

Aside from those homes, businesses, and government institutions that fly Old Glory every day, the occasions for the rest of us to show our pride and patriotism are many throughout the year. But these few years since 9/11/01, occasions and celebrations have taken on new meaning in the midst of so many major events, those sad happenings at home and abroad. Desire, and the need to fly our nations's flag, has become less than occasional since the devastating attacks of 9/11, right up to and including the recent death of one of our great Presidents, Ronald Reagan. Out of pride and patriotism for our country Old Glory flies in support of those who have or who are serving in our armed forces; she flies out of honor and respect for those who have died fighting for our freedom to live in this great country; she flies during sadness or in great jubilation; she flies because ... because the greatness and goodness we have in this country far surpasses that of any other in the world.

Because of a simple request the other day, this column is devoted to the American Flag. What follows next is not new, the author is unknown, but it has been floating about on the internet of late and is well worth the read.

I AM THE FLAG OF THE UNITED STATES OF AMERICA.
MY NAME IS OLD GLORY.

I FLY ATOP THE WORLD'S TALLEST BUILDINGS,
I STAND WATCH IN AMERICA'S HALLS OF JUSTICE.

I FLY MAJESTICALLY OVER GREAT INSTITUTIONS OF LEARNING.
I STAND GUARD WITH THE GREATEST MILITARY POWER IN THE WORLD.
LOOK UP AND SEE ME!!!

I STAND FOR PEACE, HONOR, TRUTH AND JUSTICE.
I STAND FOR FREEDOM!!!

I AM CONFIDENT, I AM ARROGANT, I AM PROUD.
WHEN I AM FLOWN WITH MY FELLOW

BANNERS,
MY HEAD IS HELD A LITTLE HIGHER,
MY COLORS A LITTLE TRUER.

I BOW TO NO ONE!!!!

I AM RECOGNIZED ALL OVER THE WORLD.

I AM WORSHIPED - I AM SALUTED - I AM RESPECTED - I AM REVERED.

I AM LOVED - I AM FEARED!!!

FOR MORE THAN 200 YEARS, I HAVE FOUGHT EVERY BATTLE OF EVERY WAR; GETTYSBURG, SHILOH, APPOMATTOX, SAN JUAN HILL, THE TRENCHES OF FRANCE, THE ARGONNE FOREST, ANZIO, ROME, THE BEACHES OF NORMANDY, THE JUNGLES OF GUAM, OKINAWA, TARAWA, KOREA, VIETNAM, THE HEAT OF THE PERSIAN GULF,
AND A SCORE OF OTHER PLACES.......

LONG FORGOTTEN BY ALL, BUT THOSE WHO WERE THERE WITH ME.

I WAS THERE!!!

I LED MY SAILORS AND MARINES.

I FOLLOWED THEM, I WATCHED OVER

THEM, THEY LOVED ME.

I WAS ON A SMALL HILL ON IWO JIMA.

I WAS DIRTY, BATTLE TORN AND TIRED,
BUT MY SAILORS AND MARINES CHEERED
ME!!!

I WAS PROUD!!!

I HAVE BEEN SOILED, BURNED, TORN AND
TRAMPLED
ON IN THE STREETS OF OTHER COUNTRIES
THAT I HAVE HELPED TO SET FREE.
IT DOES NOT HURT, FOR I AM INVINCIBLE.

I HAVE BEEN SOILED, BURNED, TORN AND
TRAMPLED ON
IN THE STREETS OF MY OWN COUNTRY.
AND WHEN IT IS DONE BY THOSE WHOM
WITH I HAVE SERVED IN BATTLE,
IT HURTS!!!

BUT I SHALL OVERCOME, FOR I AM
STRONG!!!

I HAVE SLIPPED THE SURLY BONDS OF
EARTH,
AND FROM MY VANTAGE POINT ON THE
MOON,
I STAND WATCH OVER THE NEW FRONTIERS
OF SPACE.

I HAVE BEEN A SILENT WITNESS TO ALL OF
AMERICA'S FINEST HOURS,
MY FINEST HOUR COMES WHEN I AM TORN
INTO STRIPS TO BE USED AS BANDAGES
FOR MY WOUNDED COMRADES ON THE
FIELD OF BATTLE,
WHEN I FLY HALF MAST TO HONOR MY
SAILORS AND MARINES,
AND WHEN I LIE IN THE TREMBLING ARMS
OF A GRIEVING MOTHER AT THE GRAVESITE
OF HER FALLEN SON OR DAUGHTER.

I AM PROUD!!!

MY NAME IS OLD GLORY.
LONG MAY I WAVE, DEAR GOD, LONG MAY
I WAVE!!!

When people are draping their flags, are they doing it according to the U.S. Flag Code? To follow are proper flag handling tips according to the U.S. Flag Code:
* The U.S. flag should not be displayed in bad weather unless it's made of nylon or other non-absorbent material. Today, however, most flags are made of all-weather materials.
* Only the President of the United States or a state governor can order a flag to be flown at half-staff. This gesture is an indication of national mourning.
* If the U.S. flag isn't flown from a staff, it should be displayed vertically, indoors or out, and suspended so that its folds fall free. The stripes can be displayed either horizontally or vertically, as long as the union is uppermost

and to the flag's own right.

* Any unserviceable flag should be destroyed by burning it. Many American Legion posts conduct Disposal of Unserviceable Flag ceremonies on June 14, Flag Day.

* A flag can be washed or dry-cleaned depending on the material.

* The U.S. flag should not touch anything beneath it, such as the ground. This provision is so the flag does not become dirty. It is not a requirement to destroy it if it does.

* A person other than a veteran can have his or her casket draped with the U.S. Flag, although the honor is usually reserved for veterans or state and national figures.

* The Flag Code states that flags should only be displayed from sunrise to sunset when out in the open. The flag may be displayed 24-hours a day only if it's properly illuminated.

* The U.S. flag flies over the White House when the President is in Washington, D.C. It is not displayed when the President is traveling.

* The flag should never be used as a covering for a ceiling.

* The flag should never have placed upon it, nor on any part of it, nor attached to it any mark, insignia, letter, word, figure, design, picture or drawing of any nature.

* The flag never should be used for advertising purposes in any manner whatsoever. It should not be embroidered on such articles as cushions or handkerchiefs and the like, printed or otherwise impressed on paper napkins or boxes or anything that is designed for temporary use and discard. Advertising signs should not be fastened to a staff or halyard from which the flag is flown.

* No part of the flag should ever be used as a costume

[patches are acceptable]. The flag represents a living country and is itself considered a living thing. Therefore, the lapel flag pin, being a replica, should be worn on the left lapel near the heart.

Be proud and respectful of our nation's flag, Old Glory. She stands for our fallen, our servicemen and women, and freedom for all.

Writers Note:

Thank you Mariam Graham for your suggestion. For more information on flag etiquette or the official U.S. Flag Code visit the American Legion website at www.legion.org.

If you enjoyed this story and have a story and/or some old photographs of your own about Cooke County, please contact or E- Mail Timothy L. Parks at the University of North Texas at ParksT @adaf.admin.unt.edu. or call 940-612-0202.

Patriotism and support of our troops shown in the display of magnetic ribbons attached to vehicles.

© 2004 Timothy L. Parks

Through Rain, Sleet, or Snow

On his present route, Kevin Norris of The United States Postal Service.
© 2004 Timothy L. Parks

Through Rain, Sleet, or Snow

The year was 1989, it was mid May, and for the first time ever in his postal career, Kevin Norris was called in without completing delivery of the U.S. Mail. His route at that time was on the east side of Gainesville.

"I was at a mailbox delivering the mail", Kevin tells me speaking of that morning in May. "I saw in my rearview mirror this pickup, it just comes out of nowhere. It's kind of like in the movies, you just see it suddenly appear. To describe it to you, it was raining so hard I could not have seen you across this table. It was my supervisor in the truck, Fred Eichenberger, our postmaster at the time was Merle Curry.

"You were just continuing your route even though you couldn't see more than five feet in front of you?", I asked.

"Timothy, I was going to keep on doing it."

Through rain, sleet, or snow so the saying goes ... but they didn't bother to mention floods, did they?"

"No, they didn't mention floods."

"Did you know that it was flooding?

"It was so bad Timothy, in the part of town along Rosedale, the streets in Fairview Subdivision had water running from curb to curb. This is a relatively high part of town. It was raining so hard it was extremely dangerous. This was the only time I've ever been on my route and they actually curtailed the mail -- told me to go back to the post office. To this day, I don't see how they found me. I really don't."

"What flooded?," I asked. "Was it the Elm Fork or Pecan Creek?"

"Pecan Creek and the river, both of them", said Kevin.

As it was in the flood of '81, so it was in the flood eight years later. A swath, about two blocks to the east and two blocks to the west along Pecan Creek, was overrun with water and the Elm Fork of the Trinity River went over its banks spreading into low areas on both sides of Interstate 35, including Leonard Park and Frank Buck Zoo. What rolled in as severe thunderstorms in the early hours of the morning, then turned into torrential rains that seemed like they would never end. Total rainfall recorded that day was nearly 8 inches.

"It had been raining for several days", Kevin went on, "So everything was ..."

"Saturated, like it is now", I jumped in.

"... yes, like it is now. It didn't have anywhere to go, all this rain. And it just kept raining. I mean we'd get 2 or 3 inches in an hour - it was that kind of a rain. Hard, steady, steady, steady rain. A tropical type of rain."

It was late in June - last month that Kevin and I

spoke of the flood of '89. It had been wet, in fact close to record rainfall had fallen so that conditions were ripe for flooding if heavy rains were to come in a short amount of time. They never did fortunately, although minor flooding had already occurred.

"They came and got me and told me I had to follow them. We snaked our way back, did all kinds of dados, some of the streets we were actually driving along side in the yards.I made it back to the Post Office and back home, but the next day when I came to work, I exited the Interstate and here's these guys on horseback, some of them had ropes trying to lasso zoo animals. They were trying to corral them into make shift pens, into trailers. They were actually out there ropin' deer, there were zebras running around. The Holiday Inn - where the Ramada Inn is now — out there in that plain between the motel and the Interstate is all flat. They had trucks and trailers there and were trying to get the animals back across the Interstate to the zoo. There was at least one deer, a spotted deer, that had been run over on the highway."

Gerry the retired Gainesville Community Circus elephant, whom survived the 1981 flood was nowhere to be found, then discovered perched high in a tree. Did she climb up there or just by luck end up entangled in its branches above the flood waters? Perhaps a little of both. The Frank Buck Zoo was hit hard again in 1989, and experienced at this sort of thing, Gerry went for the trees. A lot of the zoo animals were loosed by the flooding waters.

Has there ever been any rains like that since the floods of '81 or '89?"

"No, nothing so intense. We're talking about rains

that lasted a week, maybe even more, then a heavy deluge on top of that."

I stopped late in the afternoon last month - it was Tuesday June 9th - and just off of exit 495 watched the waters of the swollen Elm Fork of the Trinity River with Don Moody.   His job to take measurements of the rising waters and keep adventurous, but unwary, people from driving into the water thinking they might ford the waters under the Interstate 35 bridge, make the turn around and head south on the other side. They would head south this day alright, floating south to Lake Ray Roberts of one had gotten through and tried. . Coworkers were doing the same on the other side, keeping traffic at bay, turning them back. He explained to me that much work has been done to prevent flooding of the magnitude known before. Besides, he reminded me that the floods of '81 and '89 were the product of very heavy rainfall that came all at once and on top of a very wet ground.

Some Gainesville residents survived both the flood of 81' and to their dismay survived another one in 1989. Flooding in Gainesville is not an unfamiliar event. One resident was noted in 1989 remembering a flood in 1974. Other periods of heavy rain, with flooding of some type occurred February 8th & 9th of 1966, six inches fell in 8 hours. The month of April in 1942, 16.5" was logged in for Cooke County. September 28 through October 1 of 1903 saw 10" of rain in Gainesville and earlier that year the first week of July was really wet - 14" of rain that week!

"One of the first things I heard when I came to Gainesville to work", said Kevin, "Was about the 1981 flood. Here I was, on the job a little over a year and guess what ... here it came again."

Kevin Norris, postal worker, survived the flood of '89.

Writer's Note: Thanks to Kevin Norris for his recollections, for his dedication in delivering the U.S. Mail, and thank you to Don Moody and all of Texas Department of Transportation for keeping an eye on the river this past June.

Elm Fork of the Trinity River was out of its banks on
June the 9th of this year.
© 2004 Timothy L. Parks

Don Moody with Texas Department of Transportation.
© 2004 Timothy L. Parks

MARGARET HAYS DONATES STAINED GLASS

Margaret P. Hays standing for one of the last times in her now empty
home, the house at 1312 E. Pecan no longer hers.
© 2002 Timothy L. Parks

Stained glass from the old Whaley Methodist Church donated to
The Morton Museum by Margaret Hays hangs temporarily in front of
a south facing Morton Museum window so as not to be damaged.
The window shutters will be removed, the stain glass frame sized so that it
will slip permanently into the opening of the window.

Margaret Hays Donates Stained Glass

What a treasure Margaret has been to the community, she has contributed so much - it is an enormous loss to see her leave. It was a great loss for me personally to see her leave because she had been my mentor since I moved here and went to work at the museum. ---- Shana Powell, Curator of The Morton Museum

A very nice lady, she does a lot for a lot of people. A lot of people here are going to miss her. ---- Ingrid Vasquez, Housekeeper

Gainesville will sorely miss Margaret P. Hays. Those who have known her for a long time may never go a day without some thought of her. For the ones who only came to know Margaret recently, they understand all too well they missed out on something special not having gotten know her better. Whoever it is that said you can't miss something you never had is wrong!

After so many years in Gainesville, residing at 301 E. Pecan, Margaret P. Hays has left her home. Officially she moved to Chapel Hill, North Carolina in July of this year. She came back to Gainesville mid December only to make official the sale of her house and box up what she did not move to Chapel Hill in July. She was busy but kind enough to offer up some precious time and talk.

One should not be surprised at her move, only what took so long to answer the call. The itch to travel, to change jobs or positions, the predilection to move one place to another epitomizes the first half of Margaret's life.

Finishing high school in 1929, and having taken four college courses that last year of school, she went to North Texas State Teachers College the summer of 1929. She came back to Gainesville, went to and finished junior college in the summer of 1930 then returning to North Texas State Teachers College the winter and summer of 1930 and 1931 graduating with a degree in business.

Her first job was at North Texas Teachers College (The University of North Texas) as the Register of the Demonstration School. She was there until 1942, spending most of that time working for - looking after - Dr. Harris, the Dean of the College. Speaking of Dr. Harris, Margaret recalls, "He always would introduce me whenever anybody new would come in ."

'I'd like you to meet a young lady who makes a living for five people: Mrs. Harris, our two children, me and herself.', would say Dr. Harris

"What a wonderful compliment, Dr. Harris was a wonderful person," Margaret said.   "I took one year off during that period 1933 to 1942. In 1938 and 1939 I went to Michigan and did all my course work for my masters. Then I came back to Denton.

Shortly thereafter, she went to work for the Civil Service, first assignment New Orleans. From New Orleans she went on to Buenos Aires - now in the Foreign Service - for two years, then came home and taught short hand for one semester at North Texas Sate University (The University of North Texas) in the Spring of 1945. Looking for another job, she vacillated between two job opportunities; a position, as the Dean of Woman, at the college in Nacogdoches, or to become a Vice Counsel with the Foreign Service. No surprise, she went into the Foreign Service - she was one of the first female Foreign Service officers - and went to Bogota, Columbia followed by an assignment in then Rio De Janeiro, Brazil. Because her father had died while she was in Rio, she took an assignment in Washington DC, her mother needed her and came there to live with Margaret. That was 1950 to 1954.

Achieving the level of staff Vice Counsel while in Washington she then moved on and spent two years in Manila from 1954 to 1956, followed by a stint in Mexico City from 1956 to 1958. She would loved to have stayed on longer, but instead was asked and sent back to Washington D.C. Her last assignment before retiring from the Foreign Service was in Hong Kong from 1962 to 1964. Returning again to the Foggy Bottom area near Washington D.C., to live in a house she already owned, she did research on Latin America at The American University. In August of 1966 she returned to Gainesville, for her mothers health had begun to deteriorate. She has been here ever since, until now.

Rather than travel again she moved from one community project to another here in Gainesville. Her first big project was establishing the Morton Museum. Margaret was instrumental in the founding of it, its acquisition, running it on a volunteer basis until such time the means could be found to have paid employees, and to this day is still active with it.

Before leaving she contributed one more time to "her" wonderful Morton Museum. In her home, the center pane of the west facing bay window is stained glass that came from the old Whaley Methodist Church. No longer there, the church once stood at the corner of Grand and California street; they tore it down many years ago and built a new Whaley Methodist Church located at 701 Rosedale Drive . On the bottom, listed first among other names of distinguished church members, is her father's name, Parx Or Hays - he was a Sunday School teacher there.

"The window belongs to Gainesville, it stays here", says Margaret. Hung temporarily in front of a south facing window so as not to be damaged, the window shutters behind it will be removed, the stain glass frame sized so that it will slip permanently into the opening of the window. And so it will stay forever in the Morton Museum.

In the late seventies, Margaret zeroed in on helping to acquire the soon to be closed Sante Fe Depot. When the former Mayor Glen Locke approached her with the idea of acquiring it for the city of Gainesville she climbed right on board and joined him in the pursuit. Ms. Hays was elected and served as mayor of Gainesville beginning in the spring 1981, serving one two year term. Hard work and tenacity paid off for she and the former Mayor Glen Locke. Just as he left office and Ms. Hays took oath, ownership of The Sante Fe Depot by the city of Gainesville became official.

"It took three years to get Sante Fe to donate the building to the city, and a lot of work. Somewhere along in there," says Margaret, "We formed a Community Preservation Association to have a non profit group to raise money for the depot."

For her hard work and for her many, many achievements, Margaret has been recognized numerous times. The University of North Texas recognized her as a Distinguished Alumnus in 1979. She received the "Outstanding Citizen" award for Cooke County in 1992. Morton museum goers now do their research in a research library named after her in the year 2000.

In talking quietly, reflectively and modestly about these significant milestones of her life, Margaret orated small stories of her ancestors and other people of the past, most gone now, but certainly not forgotten - by no means has Margaret forgotten. She giggles a bit as she recollects.

In one such story she spoke of the time during the Civil War when General Sherman's March came marching right up to her Granddaddy Hay's front door. "My Granddaddy Hays", she says, "Was ten years old at the time."

One of Sherman's men said to him, 'Boy, go get me that horse.'

His mother said, "Lawrence, don't you do it"

"BOY" He repeated himself, Go get me that horse.'

"Lawrence, don't you do it"

And they came to the door, they wanted food. She told them, 'Now I'll give you food, but you'll not step one foot inside that door.'

As Margaret would tell these stories her narration was soft and flowing, but when time came to quote one or more of the characters she would look away assuming that role, her manner becoming animated, her voice for example growing loud and firm as when she imitated her Great Grandmother saying, "Lawrence, don't you do it!"

Tuesday the week of December 16, Margaret permanently left her home in Gainesville. She boarded a plane and headed east returning to her new residence in Chapel Hill, North Carolina. Just a few days before she had stood in her empty home, the house no longer hers, posed for the camera and allowed a picture to made.

Already she has celebrated a birthday there in Chapel Hill turning 90 November 3rd. There is a time when age matters, matters a lot - one cannot hardly wait to grow older, become a teenager and then an adult. There is a very long spell when age moves along and of it little attention is paid until suddenly one's age is something of an enigma to all who might inquire. Ah, but then age becomes a blessing to attain quite a number of years, to have survived and done much in a lifetime while retaining relatively good health. When asked, "Any prediction Margaret, are you going to hit one hundred?"

She replied, a glint in her knowing eye, "I could ... I'd like to!"

The Georgia Bass Great Hanging Park is another community project being talked about and the planning is well underway. And yes, but of course Margaret P. Hays is involved. She formed the committee for the task; they are the best people for the job because they all have common alities regarding the civil war, the hangings, that period of time. Their ideas and opinions, however differ, and in that, the end result will be great.

About The Civil War Memorial Margaret said sure and simple, "I'm gonna get it done!"

Writer's Note:

She no longer lives here in Gainesville among us, but we have not heard the last of this exceptional woman. Ah, what a wonderful life. Gainesville already misses you Margaret P. Hays.

John Lacy Carson
Courtesy Photo

Pierce Lyndon
Courtesy Photo

Lefty

The year was 1941 when a movie entitled <u>The Apache Kid</u> was produced. Starring in the Republic film was Don "Red" Barry. Playing the character of Deputy Tom was John Cason. For the young actor from Cooke County, Texas, this was his second film and his first billed role.

John Lacy Cason was born in Cooke County July 30, 1918. Likely he was born at home on the family farm. Not unusual in those times. His father was John J. Cason, and his mother, Fannie (Johns) Cason. It was a number of years later that his birth certificate was recorded at the Cooke County Courthouse.

He arrived in Hollywood in the late nineteen thirties, but prior to bumping into an acting career he was a professional prizefighter. In Dallas, he had won a light heavy weight Golden Gloves tournament. As a professional boxer, he fought Tony Musto winning by a technical knockout. This so impressed a couple of men watching the fight they bought his contract. John was elated and humbled by this not so much because his contract had been bought, but because the new owners it turned out were George Raft and Hugh Herbert.

John's roles were almost always small and that of a bad guy, one of the henchman. Perhaps this was due to his flattened nose and a devastating left hook, both the products of his years boxing. He was widely known and credited as John Cason, but sometimes was billed as Bob Cason. Because he was left handed, on screen he was often referred to as who else, but ... Lefty.

In addition to the acting he also did stunts. Sometimes he was a stunt double. He did so for Jack Kelly in the 1957 Mavericks series and for Guy Madison in the 1951 movie *Adventures of Wild Bill Hickok*. There were others too he stood in for in that role of the unsung hero making the actor look good seemingly performing acts requiring great skill and dexterity. As important, was that any bumps or bruises would not be inflicted on the star of the show diminishing that polished, Hollywood image.

From 1941 until 1961 he was in at least 132 films. Sometimes he was credited and sometimes he was not. To name a few: He was Henchman Bart in *Ghost Guns* (1944) ... Henchman Slim in *Flame of the West* (1945) a Henchman in *South of the Chisholm Trail* (1947) ... Matt Conway in *Dead Man's Gold* (1948) ... Fred in *Traveling Saleswoman* (1950) ... Henchman in *Stage to Tucson* (1950) ... guard on train in *Texas Rangers* (1951) ... ranch owner in *Jubal* (1956) ... Seabee Metkoff in *Don't Go Near the Water* (1957). Imagine the list - 132 films!

Pierce Lyndon wrote and self published a book called, The Badmen I Rode With. He too was a henchman in a lot of films. Of John Cason he wrote ...

Bob Cason was another good fight

*man, with a few 'semi pros' behind him, and
the ridge of his nose removed to prove it.
He was one of the craziest guys I ever rode
with. He was all over the saddle on a horse.
Talk about ridin' loose - you would swear he
was going to fall off any minute. Not so, he
could really ride and cowboy, it was just his
attitude. 'Let's git and git goin.' I don't think
he ever planned anything, it was just hurry
up and get the job done.*

*He scared me once, though. We were
to ride into a bunch of trees, out of sight
and then wait for a 'shot' from the director
and come out and continue to ride. We both
barreled into the trees out of sight, pulled up
and I looked over at Bob. He was holding
his hand over his eye and between his fingers
was a small branch. It looked horrible, like
it could be driven through his eye and into his
head. I said, 'Don't move, I'll go out and kill
the shot.' And Bob says, 'No, no, wait, I think
it's alright.' He took his hand away and by
the grace of God, the stick had hit him below
the eye on the cheek bone and he caught it in
time*

*Just another freak thing that could
happen on a ride.*

And don't forget his guest appearances on television
of which there were at least ninety notable times he was
cast. Some of the shows you might have seen him in, but
just did not know who he was, were various episodes of

Wagon Train, _The Roy Rogers Show_, _The Lone Ranger_, _The Gene Autry Show_, _Annie Oakley_, _Judge Roy Bean_, _The Adventures of Kit Carson_ - the list just goes on.

John played his last role in an April 1961 episode of Wagon Train. He was Jeff. On July 7, 1961 John Lacy Cason was killed in an automobile accident near Santa Barbara, California. It is said he had been out on a hunting trip. He was 52 years old.

John was regarded by those he worked with as one of the best. Pierce Lyndon said of Cason, "He was one of the toughest in the business."

Writers Note:

I've gazed at John Cason much as I researched and wrote of him. I almost believe I remember seeing him in many an old flick. Whether I did or not, I do know I will be watching for him now in the old movies. And with television the way it is, so many of the old series being resurrected and shown again for our enjoyment, he might just show up.

Writer's Note:

I offer my thanks to Pam Baldwin, Deputy Clerk at the Cooke County Courthouse. She was so very helpful I know she spent more time assisting than she should have. I also thank Bill Riley, one of my best sources for leads about good stories regarding Cooke County.

References: Cooke County Records. A narrative on John 'Bob' "Lefty" Cason by Bobby J. Copeland. Pierce Lyndon, Tribute to a Badman, by Graham Hill.

Lash LaRue and John Cason have it out in this
lobby card for the movie *Dead Man's Gold*.
Courtesy Photo

Horse and Carriage turn of the century California Street.
The old Post Office in the foreground on the north side of
the street and the Lindsay House on the south.
Courtesy of StarrBooks

Horseless carriages diagonally parked on the north and south sides
of a 1920's California Street scene looking west.
Courtesy of StarrBooks

A cloudy day as late afternoon traffic moves along the
Old California Trail.
© 2006 Timothy L. Parks

Exterior renovations are almost complete in this August of 2006
Cooke County Courthouse photograph. Begun in 2005, the work
took a little more than a year to complete.
(c) 2006 Timothy L. Parks

Printed in the United States
59916LVS00003B/1-132

9 780977 755813